Bridge-Logos
Orlando, FL 32822 USA

Overcoming Insomnia
by Ray Comfort

Printed in the United States of America.

Library of Congress Catalog Card Number:
2006938547
ISBN#: 9780882703343

Unless otherwise indicated, Scripture quotations in this book are from the *King James Version* of the Bible.

G1.316.N.m612.35275

This book will put you to sleep!

OVERCOMING
Insomnia

Practical Help for
Those Who Suffer from
Sleep Deprivation

by Ray Comfort

Bridge Logos
Orlando, Florida 32822

Contents

Pleasant Dreams

Have you ever dreamed that you were flying and woke up with a sense of disappointment that it was just a dream? You want to get back into the same dream again but you can't, because you are grounded back in reality.

There are times when sleep can be very pleasant. There are times when a good sound sleep makes a whole night seemingly pass in a moment, leaving you refreshed and ready for the day. When that happens, sleep makes sense.

More than likely, you have picked up this book because you have lain awake at night and watched the clock. As each long hour comes around like clockwork, you became more anxious that the next day is going to be a disaster. The longer you lay awake, the less sleep you will get, and that adds up to a miserable day of feeling tired, grumpy, and being unproductive.

When lying awake through the night for hours repeats itself night after night, it can be worrisome, and that adds fuel to the fire. Worry causes sleeplessness. You have had the thought that you may never be able to get to sleep again. That one is *more* than worrisome. That's a scary thought!

Most people have had the experience of having the problems of daily living rob them of sleep. The subconscious mind runs like the main printer at the Associated Press headquarters during breaking news. Your brain keeps feeding you information you really don't want to ponder. All you want is to get to sleep!

It's been said that the best bridge between despair and hope is a good night's sleep. How true. Problems seem to go back to their true proportion after a good night's sleep. Insomnia, on the other hand, tends to exaggerate them.

Mud Hut in Africa

If you are hungry, you eat. If you are thirsty, you drink. If you are tired, you sleep. That's how it should work. You are lying in bed. You are not hungry. You are not thirsty. You are dog tired, so where then is the sleep? You are not on some cold sidewalk or in a bus shelter with newspapers for a covering to keep you warm. You are not in a mud hut in Africa with flies crawling across your face. You are not stuck for a whole night in the confined, unnatural sleeping position provided by the domestic seat of a plane. You are in your own warm bed. You have a soft pillow and clean sheets. There are no buzzing flies. It's dark. It's perfectly quiet. Why then can't you sleep?

Then it hits you! You are not *really* comfortable. You have pinpointed the problem. You turn over and snuggle into the bed. That *was* the problem. You are now perfectly at ease, waiting to drop off into the sweet world of sleep.

Back comes the breaking news story with a mass of associated and pressing thoughts. One after the other they feed your mind. You embrace them and unwittingly get caught up in the story. Suddenly you realize that you've wasted precious time thinking unwanted thoughts. You determine to forget everything that's been plaguing your tired mind.

You are not comfortable again. You need to turn over. Again! You turn over. Then you sit up for a moment and fluff the pillow. Then you pull up the covers. A few moments earlier you had flung them off.

You decide that you need to go to the bathroom, and when you get back to bed, you snuggle up. That was the problem. Any minute you will drop off to sleep. Who do you think you are kidding? Sleep isn't happening. You are wide awake.

It seems like an hour or so since you had the mud hut thoughts. You stare at the clock. Only five long minutes have passed.

The Fallen Creation
It seems that God made the day for us to do stuff, and He made the night for us to do nothing but sleep. If that's the case, the purpose of sleep seems obvious. It's to give

us rest so that when the next day dawns, we are refreshed and ready to face it and do more stuff with a renewed vigor.

Okay. It's morning. The rooster crows. The sun peeps over the horizon. You open one eye and quickly close it again. The light is painful. You open the other eye. Slowly. You made it through the night to greet another day.

Your mouth feels pasty. Your breath could kill a houseplant at twenty paces. Your eyes feel puffy and tired. You use the back of your hand to wipe away the residue of a weeping tear duct. You slowly sit up and swing your feet to the floor. Very slowly.

You sit on the side of the bed for a minute to recover from what you have just done. Your hot hands rub your tired eyes. Pieces of "sleep" fall out of them. You wipe more tears from the corners of your eyes. You slowly stand up, stretch your back, and walk to the bathroom and gaze into the mirror. You look *worse* than you feel. You must have slept on your face. There's a deep crease across your forehead. Your eyes look as though you have just done twelve rounds with Mike Tyson. Your scalp itches and your hair looks like a rejected tumbleweed.

One of the reasons that modern marriages fall apart is that many couples marry solely on looks. Hollywood epitomizes such superficiality. To assure the success of every Hollywood union, I would suggest that a comprehensive counseling course should take place during the courting process. This should be done at 6:00 AM for three consecutive mornings with the couple facing one another. No makeup. No hair brush. No breath fresheners. No acting. What you see is what you get. If they get married, that's how they are going to face each other. That's reality. That's life. If he or she can face it, then he or she should be able to face it for the rest of the marriage.

Back to the ugly sight of the morning mirror; it's not a pretty thing to behold. But it's a most necessary one. Once we see the shocking truth, the mirror sends us to the much-needed water, where we wash and get ready for the day. We hope that by the time we meet another human being we will look better, having recovered from the "refreshing" experience of sleep. What we have experienced is just one more evidence that we live in a "fallen" creation.

Let's Not Do It

If we often feel worse after the experience of sleep, why do we bother to do it? Why don't we just stay awake and enjoy more of the wonderful pleasures of this precious life? No doubt you have figured out why. It's because we can't. We are *addicted* to sleep. We have no choice in the matter. Without sleep there would be serious effects on our brain's ability to function. If you've ever gone a whole night without sleep, you will know that you end up owing a debt to sleep. You may begin by chirping through the day, but it won't be long until you hear from the debt collector. You become grumpy, groggy, irritable, forgetful, and unproductive.

After just one night without sleep, your concentration becomes more difficult and your attention span shortens. Many police officers have attested to the fact that they have pulled people over who they believed were drunk, but found that they were drivers who were merely tired.

With an extended lack of sufficient sleep, the part of the brain that controls language, memory, planning, and sense of time is severely affected, practically shutting down. A mere seventeen hours of sustained wakefulness leads to a decrease in performance that is equivalent to a blood alcohol level of 0.05 percent (that's equal to about two glasses of wine).

Research also shows that sleep-deprived individuals have difficulty in responding to rapidly changing situations and making rational judgments. This isn't good for driving, drilling your teeth, operating on your brain, or flying a 747. In real-life situations, the consequences of insomnia can sometimes be very serious. A lack of sleep is said to have been a contributory factor to a number of international disasters such as the Exxon Valdez oil spill, the horror of Chernobyl, and the Challenger shuttle explosion.

What Happens When We Sleep?

Sleep occurs in a recurring cycle of 90 to 110 minutes and has been divided into two categories. There is non-REM (this is further split into four stages) and REM sleep.

Non-REM Sleep

Stage One: Light Sleep

During the first stage of sleep, we're half awake and half asleep. It's a semi-consciousness state. Our muscle activity slows down and slight twitching may occur. Most of us have experienced strange "jumping" during this period. It's a time of light sleep from which we can be easily awakened.

Stage Two: True Sleep

After about ten minutes of light sleep, we enter stage two. This second stage lasts for about twenty minutes. The breathing pattern and heart rate begin to slow down. This period accounts for the largest segment of our sleep.

Stages Three and Four: Deep Sleep

During stage three, the brain begins to produce something called delta waves. This is a type of wave that is large (high amplitude) and slow (low frequency). Breathing and heart rate are at their lowest levels during this time.

Stage four is characterized by rhythmic breathing and limited muscle activity. If we are awakened during deep sleep, we do not adjust immediately and we often feel groggy and disoriented for several minutes after waking up. Some children experience bed-wetting, night terrors, or sleepwalking during this stage.

REM Sleep

The first rapid-eye movement (REM) period usually begins about seventy to ninety minutes after we fall asleep. We have around three to five REM episodes a night. Although we are not conscious, the brain is very active—often more so than when we are awake. This is the period when most dreams occur. Our eyes dart around (hence the name "rapid-eye movement"), and our breathing rate and blood pressure rise. However, our bodies are effectively paralyzed. This is thought to prevent us from acting out our dreams.

After REM sleep, the whole cycle begins again.

The World Record

My wife once laughed at our dog as the animal walked around in circles in its bed before she laid down. Sue stopped smiling when I reminded her of what she did before she drifted off to sleep. She gets into bed, snuggles up for a few moments, turns over to face the other way, and then turns back to her original position before drifting off to sleep. Many of us have a nightly routine. We are no different than dogs when it comes to bedding down for the night.

Like animals, we need a certain amount of sleep. A python sleeps for 18 hours every day. Tigers snooze for 15.8 hours. Domestic cats only need about 12 hours. An African elephant needs only 3.3 hours, while a giraffe survives on just fewer than two.

Most human beings need about eight hours sleep per night. In other words, the average person sleeps for about 122 days every year, and the average 75 year-old would have spent a total of about 25 years asleep.

The current world record for the longest period of time that a person has gone without sleep is an amazing 11 days. This record was set by a man named Randy Gardner in 1965. Four days into the research, he began hallucinating. This was followed by a delusion in which he thought he was a famous football player. Surprisingly, he was actually functioning quite well at the end of his research, and he could still beat a research scientist at pinball!

A Confession
We looked earlier at the fact that the Bible maintains that we live in a fallen creation. I

didn't always believe that. I believed, instead, in the theory of evolution. I had a blind faith in science, but when I asked questions as to what evidence science had for such a fantastic theory, I found that there wasn't any.

However, after many years of studying the nature of man, I have a new theory. More than once I have been awakened from a deep sleep by the sound of a loud "snort." When I have looked around to see where such a disgusting noise came from, I have found that there was no one else in the room! It is this humiliating experience that has caused me to consider that man may not have evolved from the primate after all, as evolutionists believe, but from the pig!

There is more compelling evidence for my theory. Some of us eat like pigs, while others smell like them. Human skin is akin to pig skin, and pig skin is often used in skin grafts. Then there is the evidence of homology structures. Like the pig, we have similar brains, two eyes, a mouth, a nose (snout), ears, one heart, two kidneys, a couple of lungs, red blood, a supposed tail remnant, and we both wallow in filth. When we drift into a deep sleep, we often sound like them. Ask my wife.

But there is one big difference that separates us from the bacon supply. God has placed "eternity" in the human heart. He has given each of us the ability to consider eternity. It's rushing at the world like a great freight train, but most people don't give a toot about its arrival. Eternity isn't in their immediate agenda.

So, before we look at how to stop insomnia, I want to be candid with you. I have a two-fold hope with this book. I want you to be able to get a regular good night's sleep, and at the same time I want to waken you from a deep sleep that has made you forget that you have to face eternity. I want to make you seriously consider your eternal salvation. So please be patient with me, and let me briefly reason with you about the most important of life's issues.

I trust that you have thought out the subject of human origins. We only have two options. We either have intelligent design or unintelligent design. Either God created everything—the flowers, birds, trees, the seasons, the sun, the moon, and the stars, the marvels of the human body, fruit trees, the clouds, blue skies, love, and laughter, or it all came about by accident. Those who have been given brains realize that the latter thought is unthinkable. No painting happened by accident, with no painter. No building happened by accident—with no builder, and nothing in creation happened without a Creator. That's why the Bible says that the fool has said in his heart, "There is no God." Atheistic evolution is intellectual suicide. It's also an embarrassment.

The Bible, on the other hand, is axiomatic. It is self-evident. It proves itself to be the Word of the One who created all things. It is packed with scientific and medical facts written thousands of years before man discovered them.[1] It has the fingerprints of God all over it.

I thank God for the Bible because it tells me that what we have in sleep and in the rest of this life isn't the way He planned for it to be. Think for a moment about the weather. Did God plan it to be like this? We have massive hurricanes, terrifying tornadoes, devastating floods, deadly droughts, killer tsunamis, and lightning strikes that not only kill people, but start enormous forest fires. Bad weather kills thousands of people each year. I say it with reverence—if God planned it this way, He didn't do a very good job. Doesn't He know how to control the weather He created?

Then think of all the diseases that plague humanity. There aren't hundreds of them—there are *thousands*. Did God create us to live a life of continual suffering, and then at the end of it to be swallowed by this horrifying thing called "death"? Not according to the Bible. All these things confirm what the Scriptures tell us. As I said earlier, we live in a *fallen* creation. When God made man and woman, they were perfect. There was no disease, no suffering, no pain, and there was no death. When man sinned against God, however, a couple of ugly bedfellows arrived on the scene—suffering and death.

So what about sleep? Where does that come into the equation? Is it a part of the original Genesis plan, or is it the result of the Fall?

We are told that night existed in the beginning (Genesis 1:5) and so it seems that Adam slept (unless he was a night owl). More than likely the night was a time for him to snooze. Its purpose was to rest and refresh him, and in the morning he woke up with the sweetest of breath. But when sin came, then came the curse in its trail. And with the curse came the sufferings of this life, including the curse of insomnia. It's part of the many *dis*eases that plague us. With insomnia we lose the "ease" we need to get to sleep.

The Big Question

The great genius Thomas Edison said, "We do not know one-millionth of one percent about anything." How true. This is true about why we sleep. Believe it or not, science can't even tell us why we go to sleep. Think of it. We spend a third of our precious lives doing something and we have no idea *why* we do it. Edison, the inventive genius, thought that sleep was a waste of time.

The question as to why we sleep has baffled scientists for centuries. Some believe that sleep gives the body a chance to recuperate from the day's activities, but in reality, the amount of energy saved by sleeping for even eight hours is miniscule—about the same amount of energy that is contained in a piece of toast.

As we have seen, we *have* to sleep because it is essential to maintaining normal levels of speech, memory, and innovative and flexible thinking. Without it we go nuts.

Self-induced Insomnia

I once slept under a car. This happened when I was on a surfing trip. We had arrived at a beach late at night, so I crawled under the car and went to sleep. As a teenager, I had no trouble falling asleep. It was a natural part of living.

But I was converted at the age of twenty-two, and as a new Christian, I decided to do what Jesus did. He prayed for an entire night. I determined I would do the same thing.

I started around 8:30 PM, but by midnight I felt as though I had been praying for a couple of months. I lasted until 2:00 AM and gratefully ran home to bed.

However, I was aware that if I wanted to be used by God to reach this world with the message of salvation, I *had* to pray.

It is not only biblical to be a prayer warrior, but history attests to its necessity. Men who were greatly used by God were always great men of prayer. But I had a problem. I suffered from undiagnosed ADD on steroids! I couldn't sit still for more than a few minutes. I had to be always doing something. So remaining still in prayer was very difficult for me.

I tried to deal with the problem by going on "prayer walks." Each day I would simply walk and pray. I did that for years, but around 1983, I decided that I would go to sleep, and then get up and pray, and I've been following that approach since then.

This is the routine. I have a large drink of water or juice in the evening, and when nature's alarm clock calls, I get up. This is usually between midnight and 1:00 AM. At that point I am very sleepy and the temptation to drop back into bed is overwhelming. Instead, I go into another room, grab a blanket, wrap it around myself, drop to my knees and pray in the darkness of the night.

Before I know it, thirty minutes has gone by. I turn on the light, turn on my computer, and write.

Two hours pass. I'm wide awake. I'm alert. I am vigilant. I'm keyed up. I'm in a creative mood. I'm in a perfect state of mind for not going back to sleep.

I then quietly go back into our bedroom, get into bed, snuggle up, and lie awake for three or four hours.

I toss, turn, look at the clock, mumble, look at the clock, stare at the darkness, study the inside of my eyelids, look at the clock, and think deeply about sleep. No one thinks about food like a hungry man, and no one thinks about sleep like someone who can't get any!

Sleepy Thoughts

Like Thomas Edison, I also think that sleep is a waste of time (although it can be pleasurable). But not being *able* to sleep is an even greater waste of time. It's not only unproductive to lie there awake, but not sleeping takes away the potential productivity of the next day. Instead of our battery being charged, we lie in bed unplugged, leaving us with no energy for the next day.

I'm sure Edison's thoughts about sleep were influenced by the fact that sleep puts us into a state of temporary insanity. We dream that we are flying through the clouds on the back of a green elephant, and it all seems normal and right. Normal, that is until we wake up and realize that through no desire of our own we were taken into a fantasy world and dreamed dreams of lunacy. What's more, during that time we were duped into believing such experiences were standard human behavior. If the sanest of us shared our dreams with a clinical psychologist, he would probably be able to justify having us locked up!

Then there's the "joy" of the nightmare. This phenomenon has a bedfellow called the "night terrors." The night terrors sufferer wakes up in the night terrified, but he or she isn't fully awake and often can't remember the incident in the morning. The spouse is suddenly awakened from a deep sleep by the person with this complaint, and the experience of seeing an incoherent human being with the night terrors is frightening.

No doubt you have had nightmares. They happen when a perfectly well-balanced person, who is trying to make it through life without stress, is stressed to a point of absolute and helpless terror. For no obvious reason we dream that we are falling from a plane, being buried alive, drowning, dying, being chased by a vicious murderer or a pack of hate-filled Nazis, by monsters, or hungry cannibals, or we are about to be eaten alive by wild animals, or sucked dry of our life's blood by leeches, or crushed by massive snakes. We suddenly wake up sweating like a roast pig, our poor heart thumping through our chest, hyperventilating, with a feeling of horror that is so real it takes about ten minutes to shake it off.

So-called experts tell us that we are living out our fears through our dreams. That may be so, but I don't *want* to live out my fears. I don't want to have anything to do with them!

Add to this the common complaints of waking up with a feeling of nausea or a debilitating headache, teeth-grinding during the night, sleep apnea, acid reflux, and periodic limb movement disorder.

We spend a third of this unspeakably valuable life in an involuntary state, dreaming insane and terrible dreams we don't want to dream, lying on our backs with our mouths open like the mouth of a volcano, spouting a noise that sounds like a hungry pig rummaging in a sty. Nice.

What's more, we are addicted to doing this sleeping thing night after night for our entire lives. If we woke up every morning bright and fresh as a spring daisy and raring to take on another day, it would be different. But we don't. We more than often feel worse when we wake up than when we went to sleep.

So during these times of not being able to get to sleep, I have given sleep profound thought. I even did some research on insomnia in animals because I suspected that the problem of sleeplessness was confined to human beings. I discovered an article by a man who said that his dog was barking incessantly late one night. After some time he decided that there may be a prowler in his yard, so he went out into the dark of the night to investigate. The dog kept barking continually at something in the distance, so he let the dog go and followed him.

It wasn't long until he bumped into a doctor who said that he was out walking because he couldn't sleep. He looked at the dog and said, "Insomnia." The doctor then said that he had something to help with the canine's problem, and gave him some medicine. The animal immediately stopped barking and went to sleep.

At this point I decided that I had been completely wrong about insomnia being confined to human beings. I decided to let sleeping dogs lie, and not pursue the thought. But I read on and found that the sleeping medicine worked well. Too well.

The next morning a man came and picked the dog up by the tail and put him where daisies grow. It took me a minute to realize that the neighbor had poisoned the dog—that was causing his insomnia.

The ending of the story did strengthen my suspicion that animals have no trouble falling to sleep. Think about it for a moment. Does your dog or cat walk around all night, not able to sleep? It seems that the whole animal kingdom has no trouble in that area. If there are night owls, they are night owls because they were made that way.

Why then do human beings have trouble falling asleep? What do we possess that the animal kingdom doesn't have? One answer is that we are made with the capacity to *reason*. I think, therefore I am. We think, create, discover, and we appreciate. We write music and form ourselves into orchestras. We dream and discover distant lands. We imagine and then invent. We care about right and wrong and form justice systems. We appreciate a sunset and a rose. We understand that we are mortal, and we think about eternity. We are able to experience humor, and laugh at life. Animals don't do these things.

We have more than just an animal instinct to survive. And therein we find the problem. Our brain is far more complex than that of an animal. We think. We reason. We worry. We think, reason, and worry too much, and it is the complexity of our brain activity that keeps us awake.

It is because of my frustration with the inability to sleep that I have done more than most to fight the Battle of Insomnia:

• Many years ago I produced and armed myself with an audio called "Yawnese." This was sixty minutes of pure, genuine, non-stop yawns. Some things in life are contagious. One is laughter. Have you ever stood with a group of people who are laughing at a joke you didn't hear? You find yourself laughing along with them and yet you don't know what's so funny. This is the principle behind laugh-tracks on TV shows. The audience laughs at things that wouldn't normally crack a smile on a bullfrog and you find yourself joining in. It makes us think that we are enjoying the program.

The same contagious principle applies to yawning. Even the word "yawn" tends to make us want to yawn, so I figured that if I played the Yawnese tape it would make me want to go to sleep. It made me yawn, but it didn't put me to sleep.

• I searched the Internet for audios of boring preachers preaching boring sermons. Charles Spurgeon, one of the most electrifying preachers in history, said, "There are brethren in the ministry whose speech is intolerable; either they dun you to death, or else they send you to sleep. No chloral can ever equal their discourse in sleep-giving properties. No human being, unless gifted with infinite patience, could long endure to listen to them, and nature does well to give the victim deliverance through sleep."

I couldn't find any boring preachers preaching boring sermons. It suddenly dawned on me that no one thought dull preachers were worth recording. It was a pity, because I was sure that nature would have given me deliverance through them.

• Like most men, I go into a daze when I am handed an instruction book. Instruction books are a last resort. They are where you look when the appliance doesn't work. Screeds of boring information make me want to go to sleep. Or so I thought, until I deliberately took a huge computer instruction book to bed in an effort to send myself off into the Land of Nod. That didn't work either.

• I have tried drinking warm milk. That didn't work.

• I tried to think of nothing. That's impossible. Try it. The thought, "Okay ... I'm thinking of nothing, now what?" stops you from thinking about nothing.

• I have watched TV until my eyes ached. That just fed my mind with more information to think about.

• I have burned off energy through exercise. That left me tired, exhausted, and awake.

• I have listened to talk radio—more food for thought.

• I have listened to the Bible on CD, in the hope that I would get bored and drop off. I found that other thoughts tended to crowd in and keep me awake. Nothing worked.

• And of course, I counted sheep until I got tired of looking at them.

The Power of Distraction

My problem with insomnia was self-induced. My mind was racing at 100 MPH because I had filled it with gas and set it in gear. I had to find the brakes. But how do you stop a speeding mind? You can, if you have a mind to.

I have noticed something interesting about sleep. It often comes to us when we don't want it to. Take, for instance, a problem I have of nodding off in church. Sometimes I find myself sitting in a pew listening to a preacher, and what he is saying doesn't exactly grip me. It's not the preacher's fault. Remember, I have ADD on steroids. Suddenly I find an irresistible urge to go to sleep. Nature is trying to give me relief. I can't figure out why, because I wasn't at all tired when I entered the building. It's not stuffy so I can't blame the atmosphere. Being a preacher, I'm aware that if I can see the preacher, he can see me. I don't want to discourage him by sleeping during his sermon. I don't want to embarrass my wife by snoring. After a battle, the overwhelming urge to fall asleep leaves. Phew, I beat it.

Then I get nudged by Sue and hear her whisper, "You're going to sleep!" Huh? I thought I had overcome that. I shake myself out of it once again, and zero in on what's being said from the pulpit. I make myself concentrate once again on what's being communicated by the preacher.

Suddenly I hear Sue firmly whisper, "*You're going to sleep again!*" The more I try and concentrate on what is being said from the pulpit, the easier it is for sleep to overtake me ... *and there's the key to beating insomnia.*

I go to sleep in church—a place where I *want* to stay awake, and yet I stay awake in bed, a place where I want to go to sleep. *Why is that?*

Here is the reason. It is because I am deliberately stilling my subconscious mind of all other distracting thoughts. That's what makes the way for sleep to take over the human mind.

Have you ever had a small child in your arms, and he's screaming because he skinned his knee? To him, it's a major disaster. He can't think of anything else but the hurt. So you distract him. You ask, "Did you see that cat over there?" The child stops screaming, and looks at the cat. The distraction stills him. It takes his mind off the pain.

That's what we can do with a mind that is screaming with thought, and won't still itself. We can *distract* it of thought. In doing so, we do what I was doing in church. I was so concerned about the embarrassment of going to sleep, I pushed all other thoughts out of my mind, and this made the way for sleep to do its thing. Here are two ways to do that outside of sitting in church:

1. Listen For a Distant Noise

You may not be able to tune into a distant preacher, but you can perhaps listen to birds singing, for cars on a freeway, or if you live in the country, the sound of croaking frogs or crickets. To concentrate on listening, you will have to put every other thought aside for a moment. I have done this many times, and it does work. However, there are often times when it doesn't work, because it's not easy to do. It takes a lot of concentration. Many a time I have listened for a distant noise, zeroed in on it, and before I knew it I found myself once again thinking thoughts at 100 MPH.

2. Counting Backwards

Another way to still the mind is to distract it by counting backwards from 100. Again, this does work, but it takes a great deal of self-discipline because your mind will get bored and other thoughts will crowd in. I have lost count of the times I have counted backwards and unconsciously crossed over to other thoughts before I even got to the number 80. Counting sheep uses the same principle but this rarely works for me, because the fluffy animals won't stand still!

There is a better way. We will look closely at that in the next chapter.

The Missing Information

By far the most effective way to still an active mind so that the process of sleep can take over is through good, old-fashioned reading. I am aware that most insomniacs have tried reading and it doesn't work, but that's because they are missing some important information. The process of sleep comes in *waves*. It's vital that you understand this if you want to conquer insomnia.

You may have noticed that daily human bodily functions come in waves. They come in "urges" that peak, go away for a short time, and then return some time later. The same thing happens with labor contractions. A woman in labor will find that there is a wave of unbearable pain. It subsides for a time. Then another wave comes a few moments later, the distance between them depending on how close she is to childbirth. And that's how the body works when it comes to the urge to sleep.

You are lying in bed. Hours have passed and you have done all the tossing and turning you want to do. You are physically tired, but you are wide awake. So you turn on the bedside lamp. This isn't an ordinary lamp. It's one with a very long adjustable neck that you can twist in any direction. It also has non-heat bulb. These two functions are important if you don't want to disturb your spouse or get too hot in bed because of the close proximity of the light. This means that you can lie on one side and have the light close to you and read while still snuggled up, rather than sitting up in bed. You are ready for the moment when the sleeping process comes to you.

What you are now going to do will take a lot of self-control. It's also going to take supreme concentration. But it is worth it because it will almost certainly help you to overcome the curse of insomnia.

You are going to read. I would suggest that you spend about fifteen minutes reading the Book of Psalms; then pick up a good book. It must be one that holds your interest. Again, most insomniacs have tried reading, and it doesn't work for them. This is because they are subconsciously screaming, "I really don't want to read this book ... *I just want to get some sleep!*" So what you are reading *must* hold your interest or you will become bored and stop reading before the "contractions" start coming.

Boredom will not put you to sleep. Remember, when I drifted off to sleep in church, it wasn't because I was bored. I was focused. My concentration was on the preacher because I didn't want to discourage him or to embarrass Sue. I *wanted* to listen. So it wasn't the fact that the preacher was boring that put me to sleep. It wasn't a stuffy atmosphere. It was the fact that I deliberately emptied my mind of other thoughts and zeroed in on what he was saying. So you must have a book in your hand that isn't boring. It should be a publication you are enjoying. I mistakenly thought that I could bore myself by reading a computer instruction manual.

That didn't work. All that happened when I read it was that my mind wandered onto other things. *Instead, I should have been reading a book that captivated me enough for me to rid my mind of other thoughts.* That's what would have opened me to the process of sleep.

You may read for thirty minutes, or it may be longer. You are going to read until your mind begins to *lose* the power to concentrate. *I don't mean that your mind will wander to other thoughts.* Nor do I mean that your eyes will become tired. I mean that you will experience a loss of the *ability* to concentrate because of what is happening in your brain. You won't be able to focus on a sentence. Again, this is different than having tired eyes. *It's important that you know the difference so that you will recognize it when it comes.* The sentence you are looking at will not only blur, but you won't be able to understand its meaning. This is because you lose the capability to think. Your brain has become tired.

When this happens, you must fight it. Don't stop reading! Hold onto the book and hold onto your focus. Try and read the sentence again. If you can't keep focus, hold your gaze and stay with it until the focusing ability comes back. It will, after the wave leaves. It may be two to fifteen seconds until the capability to concentrate returns.

You have just resisted the first wave of sleep. Keep reading. *Don't put the book down.* Even if you desperately want to, don't put it down. If you put it down now you will turn the light off and you may lie awake for hours. Do you want that to happen? Of course you don't. So be patient. Keep reading and wait for the second wave to come to you. It should come in three to fifteen minutes. It may take a little longer. But again, be patient.

You may be able to hasten the wave by deliberately and methodically reading each word aloud in your mind, rather than speed-reading. Look at each word like someone who is learning to read. What you are doing is attempting to exhaust your mind of its thought energy. You want to bring it to a point of not being able to take in any more information. As this happens, you may find that the book drops while you are holding it. This may startle you, but get a grip, and keep reading until a second wave comes.

When this happens—when the blurring starts, shut the book, turn the light off, turn over if you wish, and close your eyes.

Again, the key is to drain the mind. If you can do this, sleep will almost certainly ensue when the third wave comes.

There are no drugs involved. No counting sheep. No counting backwards. No computer manuals. No milk. No listening for distant noises. No yawnese tapes. No boring preachers. It is just a matter of tiring out the mind until it can't process information and shuts down by itself. All it can then do is surrender and welcome the joy of natural sleep.

Earlier in this book I said how, if we revealed our dreams, we could be deemed insane. Here's a dream I had while writing this book. It's one of my more sane ones, so I don't mind revealing it. After I finished writing this chapter, I went back to our bedroom and quietly turned on my bed lamp.

I had previously twisted the adjustable neck downwards and away from the bed so that Sue wouldn't be disturbed by the light. Then I crawled into bed, read some Psalms, and then picked up a good book. After about fifteen minutes, the first wave of sleep came. I resisted it. When the second one came a few minutes later, I put the book down, turned off the light and went to sleep.

Suddenly there were about eight black, ten-inch "helicopter" bugs flying towards me (this was nuts because I have never even seen ten-inch helicopter bugs!). When a couple of them landed on my head, I had had enough. I shouted something in protest and that woke me up.

My first reaction was to stress out. I had gone through the long and laborious process of tiring my mind; it had worked, and now some stupid dream had ruined everything just minutes after I had drifted off to sleep. Now I was wide awake, but instead of letting it stress me, I recalled that a few moments earlier I had exhausted my mind. It should, therefore, still be exhausted. So, I disciplined myself not to think about the dream. That was the last thing I remember thinking until the morning.

The Same Principle
The insomniac may think that staying awake is a real pain, but falling asleep at the wrong time can be even more painful. According to the US Department of Transportation an estimated 100,000 accidents are caused each year by drowsiness and fatigue. These result in about 1500 deaths each year. According to University of New York, Albany researchers who polled nearly 600 cross-country truck drivers at state truck stops and weigh-in stations found that nearly twenty-five percent of the drivers reported falling asleep at the wheel at least once last year, and two-thirds reported driving while drowsy in the month before they were interviewed.

The average American spends an amazing seventy-two minutes in his car every day. According to *AORN Journal* (March, 2003):

Approximately 100 million people or 51% of the US adult driving population are driving while drowsy, and nearly 14 million people have fallen asleep at the wheel in the past year, according to a November 20, 2002, news release from the National Sleep Foundation. The foundation's annual Sleep in America poll also revealed that 1% of drivers have had an accident because they were driving when drowsy or fell asleep while driving; men and young adults between the ages of 18 and 29 are at the highest risk for driving while drowsy or falling asleep at the wheel; adults with children are more likely to drive while drowsy compared to adults without children; and adults 65 years of age and older are least likely to drive while drowsy or fall asleep while driving.

Again, here we see the same principle that we have studied. If statistics about how many millions suffer from sleeplessness hold true, many of these people who are falling asleep at the wheel are insomniacs. They have trouble going to sleep when they want to, but fall asleep when they don't want to. This is because they are tired and they are trying desperately to concentrate on driving. Remember, they are focusing on *one* subject—driving, and it is the stilling of the mind of other thought that paves the way for the sleeping process. Tragically, many wake up dead!

An Expert s Advice

If you search for "cures" for insomnia, you will find all sorts of advice. Here's some from an expert. In the light of the principle we just looked at, see why what he is saying may work:

> Deep physical relaxation can greatly enhance your ability to fall asleep when you want and to stay asleep once you are there. Follow these directions and you will become deeply relaxed.
>
> Lie down and get comfortable. Close your eyes and do some deep breathing to get rid of your surface tension. Next, visualize or imagine that you have tiny faucets at the end of each finger and at the end of each toe. The faucets are all turned on and all the stress and tension in your body is draining out through these faucets. Feel it happening as you watch the stress and tension running out of the faucets. Now, concentrate on your feet and imagine that the muscles of your feet are becoming as loose and limp as a cooked piece of spaghetti. Spend a few

minutes focusing on your feet and let them relax. Don't try to make it happen. Focus on that cooked piece of spaghetti and just let your muscles go. They will relax. Next, concentrate on the muscles of your calves. Spend a few minutes there and let them relax. Then focus on your thighs and let them relax. Work up your body letting each part relax. Relax your buttocks, stomach, chest, back, shoulders, arms, hands, neck, head, and face.

As you relax each successive part of your body, the next part will become easier to relax. Don't rush yourself. Focus on your muscles becoming just as loose and limp as that cooked piece of spaghetti. As you do, your body will drift into a deep state of physical relaxation. If you are not already asleep, you will be able to drift asleep at this point.

The problem with most insomniacs isn't a restless body. It's their restless *mind*. Their tired body is exhausted. After being up for a couple of hours at night I am physically tired. That's why I decide to go back to bed. As I sit in front of my computer screen, my eyes burn. I find myself yawning. The involuntary action takes place because I am not drawing enough oxygen into my lungs, so the body takes over and does what I am too physically tired to do. Again, I am not mentally, but physically tired. I am *longing* to drop off into the realm of sleep. I *crawl* between the sheets.

It's not long before I begin my tossing and turning. But if I dropped off to sleep within a few minutes, I wouldn't be conscious of any of that. The problem is that we mistake tossing and turning for restlessness. But the continual activity that happens while awaiting sleep isn't because of a *physical* restlessness;[2] we have already established that I am exhausted. It's because of a natural physical function.

Someone who has leprosy is not able to feel pain. That may sound like a blessing, but it's not. Because there is no feeling, the leper will sit down for a while and will not feel the urge to every now and then shift around on his or her buttocks. A normal person will feel uncomfortable and move a little. The reason a healthy person instinctively moves around is so that blood can flow through the flesh. If this isn't allowed to happen, the skin will rot and become leprous. That's why we shift about all night when we are asleep. The average person tosses and turns all night.

While the expert's advice about focusing on different parts of your body and thinking limp thoughts about them may help you to physically relax, what you are actually doing is focusing the *mind* on an activity. Again, it is when the mind is stilled of all other thought that makes a way for sleep to come in, rather than imagining yourself as a limp piece of spaghetti.

Here's the Killer!

When I was a child, I remember trying to watch for the moment that I went to sleep. I would lie awake on my bed and wait for the very second when my eyelids would come down. I wanted to witness the moment when I went to sleep, but I never saw it. Not once. I would diligently watch. The next thing I knew it was morning, and I would say to myself, "I missed it again!"

The reason I didn't see the moment I went to sleep was because it's not the eyes that go to sleep, it's the brain. Think of what happens if you pull the TV plug out at the wall while the set is still on. The plug comes out, and then the screen shuts down. That's what happens when sleep comes along. The plug is pulled out of the conscious mind, then an instant later the screen (the eyes) shut down. You never get to see the eyes close because your brain has already gone into the sleeping mode, just before the eyes shut. You are sound asleep when the eyelids come down.

That's why so many people die at the wheel. They think that they are in control. They are tired, yes, but the eyelids coming down will be a sign to them of how tired they are. If that happens, *then* they will pull over and have a snooze. But they never see it happen! That is their fatal error. They will never see the "warning sign" of the eyelids closing because the brain shuts down *first*. It was my understanding of this simple principle that helped me to cure my insomnia.

How to Sleep in a Storm

If you are ever in doubt about whether or not the Bible is supernatural in origin, forget about the many amazing Bible prophecies. Forget about the incredible scientific and medical facts that were written thousands of years before man discovered them.[3] Simply do a quick word study on any subject.[4] Start at Genesis (1440 BC) and work your way through to the Book of Revelation, bearing in mind that these books were written over a thousand years apart. As you do so, it won't be long until you stand in awe at their continuity. You will find a *consistency* of information on the subject you study, even though what you are reading was written thousands of miles and sometimes thousands of years apart, by completely different authors. There could not have been any collaboration by the authors. This is absolute proof of divine authorship.[5]

Consistency in the Bible certainly is the case with the subject of sleep. If you do a word search through the Scriptures, you will find that the first time sleep is mentioned is in the context of a "deep sleep" into which God put Adam. It also speaks of something each of us has no doubt at one time experienced—a "sweet sleep." (See Proverbs 3:24 and Jeremiah 31:26.)

Another consistency is seen in that the word "sleep" is continually synonymous with the word "death." David, who wrote in 800 BC) says, "Consider and hear me, O Lord my God: lighten mine eyes, *lest I sleep the sleep of death*" (Psalm 13:3, italics mine).

Look at how the Book of Daniel (164 BC) uses the same language as it speaks of the resurrection of the dead: "And many of them that *sleep in the dust of the earth shall awake*, some to everlasting life, and some to shame and everlasting contempt" (Daniel 12:2, italics mine).

In the New Testament (written around AD 70[6]), when Jesus speaks of going to visit His friend Lazarus, look at how He speaks of death as being a "sleep." "Our friend Lazarus sleepeth; but I go, that I may awake him out of sleep. Then said his disciples, Lord, if he sleep, he shall do well. Howbeit Jesus spake of his death: but they thought that he had spoken of taking of rest in sleep" (John 11:11-13).

Then, further on in the New Testament, when the Apostle Paul speaks of the resurrection of the dead in a number of places, he also uses the word "sleep" as a synonym for death. He said, "Behold, I shew you a mystery; We shall not all sleep, but we shall all be changed" (1 Corinthians 15:51).

He also wrote, "But I would not have you to be ignorant, brethren, concerning them which are asleep, that ye sorrow not, even as others which have no hope. For if we believe that Jesus died and rose again, even so them also which sleep in Jesus will God bring with him. For this we say unto you by the word of the Lord, that we which are alive and remain unto the coming of the

Lord shall not prevent them which are asleep. For the Lord himself shall descend from heaven with a shout, with the voice of the archangel, and with the trump of God: and the dead in Christ shall rise first" (1 Thessalonians 4:13-16).

He Who Snoozes Wins

Perhaps you are familiar with the story of Peter when he nodded off while he was sitting on the brink of death. See if you can figure why he could sleep while he was awaiting execution:

"Now about that time Herod the king stretched forth his hands to vex certain of the church. And he killed James the brother of John with the sword. And because he saw it pleased the Jews, he proceeded further to take Peter also. (Then were the days of unleavened bread.) And when he had apprehended him, he put him in prison, and delivered him to four quaternions of soldiers to keep him; intending after Easter to bring him forth to the people. Peter therefore was kept in prison: but prayer was made without ceasing of the church unto God for him. And when Herod would have brought him forth, the same night Peter was sleeping between two soldiers, bound with two chains: and the keepers before the door kept the prison. And, behold, the angel of the Lord came upon him, and a light shined in the prison: and he smote Peter on the side, and raised him up, saying, Arise up quickly. And his chains fell off from his hands. And the angel said to him, Gird thyself, and bind on thy sandals. And so he did. And he saith unto him, Cast thy garment about thee, and follow me. And he went out, and followed him; and wist not that it was true which was done by the angel; but thought he saw a vision. When they were past the first and the second ward, they came to the iron gate that leadeth unto the city; which opened to them of his own accord: and they went out, and passed on through one street; and forthwith the angel departed from him. And when Peter was come to himself, he said, Now I know of a surety, that the Lord hath sent his angel, and hath delivered me out of the hand of Herod, and from all the expectation of the people of the Jews" (Acts 12:1-11).

Prior to this, Stephen had been stoned to death for preaching the Gospel. James had been murdered by Herod. Now Peter was arrested and chained to two guards. It was obvious that he was in mortal danger. The believers had an all-night prayer meeting for him. Now there's a reason for Peter to be anxious. But he slept. How could he?

Here's why. When someone is a Christian, God promises that whatever life throws at them, He will turn to their good. Here's the promise: "And we know that all things work together for good to them that love God, to them who are the called according to his purpose" (Romans 8:28).

Peter was called according to the purpose of God, and so he knew that whatever happened to him, in life or in death, God would work to his good. So he didn't lie awake worrying about his situation. He cleared his mind of all that information, and let sleep have its course. True faith in God produces true peace of mind—"Thou wilt keep him in perfect peace, whose *mind* is stayed on thee" (Isaiah 26:3, italics mine).

Jesus said that we shouldn't be concerned about the cares of this world because God will take care of those who love Him. Look at how the mind is kept in peace when we rid ourselves of worry: "Be careful for nothing; but in every thing by prayer and supplication with thanksgiving let your requests be made known unto God. And the peace of God, which passeth all understanding, shall keep your hearts and *minds* through Christ Jesus" (Philippians 4:6-7, italics mine).

We see that same thing happening with Jesus. Look at His situation and then look at the result of faith in God: "And when he was entered into a ship, his disciples followed him. And, behold, there arose a great tempest in the sea, insomuch that the ship was covered with the waves: but he was asleep. And his disciples came to him, and awoke him, saying, Lord, save us: we perish. And he saith unto them, Why are ye fearful, O ye of little faith? Then he arose, and rebuked the winds and the sea; and there was a great calm. But the men marvelled, saying, What manner of man is this, that even the winds and the sea obey him!" (Matthew 8:23-27).

Jesus slept during a storm that terrified the disciples. They were fear-full because they weren't faith-full.

Back to Sleeping Peter

It seems that Peter slept because he trusted that God was in control. The Bible says, "It is vain for you to rise up early, to sit up late, to eat the bread of sorrows: for so he giveth his beloved sleep" (Psalm 127:2).

Let me ask you perhaps the most important question you will ever be asked. Are you part of God's "beloved"? Most would quickly say that they are. They think that we are all God's children and therefore we are automatically His beloved. But the Bible doesn't say that. It tells us that we are not children of God, but children of the devil.[7]

More than likely you are reading this book because you have had trouble sleeping or you know someone in that predicament. Obviously, to get this far you are not offended by my speaking about the things of God. Perhaps you are a Christian. But I want to make sure you are soundly "saved," if you will let me. This is because experience has shown me that there are millions of people who think they are Christians, and they are not. The Bible warns that many will stand before God and expect Heaven, but they will end up in hell.[8] That is a most terrible thought, so let's do a quick test:

1. Do you love God with all of your heart? Is Jesus *precious* to you?

2. Do you read your Bible daily?

3. Are you living in holiness (separation from sin and from the world)?

4. If I ask those closest to you what you love most, will they say without any hesitation that it is God?

5. What do you pray about? Are your prayers unselfish?

6. Do you love other Christians and long to be with them?

7. Do you have a concern for those whom the Bible calls "unsaved"?

Let me explain why I have asked those seven questions. Until we are converted, we don't love God. I know that most people think they do, but the truth is that they love their *concept* of God. Having our own image of God is called "idolatry," and idolaters will not inherit the Kingdom of God. The Bible says that no one seeks after the true God:

"The Lord looked down from heaven upon the children of men, to see if there were any that did understand, and seek God. They are all gone aside, they are all together become filthy: there is none that doeth good, no, not one" (Psalm 14:2-3).

When we are converted, our relationship to God radically changes. He writes His Law upon our hearts, and the essence of His Law is that we love Him with all of our heart, mind, soul, and strength, and that we love our neighbor as ourselves. Have you had that change of heart? Have you been "born again"?[9] If you have, then you will naturally love God more than anything else, including your loved ones. God gave those you love to you—they are the gift and He is the Giver. To set your affections on the gift above the Giver of the gift is what's known as "inordinate affection," and this is a violation of the first of the Ten Commandments.

The unmistakable sign that you have been regenerated by God is that you will love

Jesus. The indwelling Holy Spirit will guide you to Him. (See John 15:26.) Do you love Jesus? Is He precious to you? "If any man love not the Lord Jesus Christ, let him be Anathema Maranatha" (1 Corinthians 16:22). How then do you show that you love Jesus? It will be evidenced by the fact that you will keep His commandments. (See John 14:21.)

So if you love God, you will read His Word. You will meditate on it day and night. You will rejoice over His promises like one who "finds great spoil." You will show that you love Him by separating yourself from that which displeases Him. "Ye adulterers and adulteresses, know ye not that the friendship of the world is enmity with God? Whosoever therefore will be a friend of the world is the enemy of God" (James 4:4).

If you are in an unconverted state or you are a false conversion (and there are millions), your prayers will be selfish. You will seek His blessing on everything you own and do, rather than seek His will. That means that you won't pray for the "unsaved."

I was on a plane once, sitting next to an elderly couple from India. During the flight, as I made my way back from the restroom, I noticed that the man's wife was also heading for the restroom. Then I saw her husband standing in the aisle, so I said to him, "If you are looking for your wife, she stepped out the back door for some fresh air."

He then mumbled (in a deep Indian accent), "Why do you think I am looking so happy?"

Of course, he was joking. Earlier, I had listened to him share his beliefs on the afterlife. Predictably, he believed in reincarnation, so I asked, "If people are dying and coming back as something else or someone else in an endless cycle, how is it that in recent years there are *billions* of new people on the earth? If we are all reincarnations, what's going on with all the new folks?"

He seemed stumped by such a thought. After we had looked closely at the Ten Commandments, he asked, "What do you pray about?" I said that I prayed that people like him would have an open heart to the Gospel, that God would give me wisdom, and that He would protect my family.

He then said, "You are a good man." I knew what he was saying. The content of my prayers confirmed the genuineness of my faith. Even a non-Christian knows that something is wrong if our prayers are selfish.

If you are in an unconverted state, you won't long to be with other Christians. Yet love for others who are converted is one sign that you have truly been regenerated by the Holy Spirit: "We know that we have passed from death unto life, because we love the brethren. He that loveth not his brother abideth in death" (1 John 3:14).

If you have looked at the above list and you are questioning your salvation, there's a terrible error into which you could now fall. You may see that you lack these things, so you begin to *do* them. You begin to read your Bible, pray unselfish prayers, etc. But these things aren't what you do to be saved. You will do them *if* you are saved.

More than likely the problem is that you lack understanding of the true nature of your sin. Please stay with me, because in the next chapter, we are going to take a look into a mirror, and it will be a most beneficial experience.

Awake, You Who Sleep

The reason why so many people sit in the shadow of death is because they have never seen the light. They may believe in God. They may go to church. They may even profess to be born again and love the Lord, but if they don't have "the things that accompany salvation," they are not saved.

Perhaps you are in one of those categories. You need light. You are asleep in your sins. Like Peter, you are on the brink of eternity, and there has been no concern as to your terrible plight. If that's you, then this verse is applicable: "Wherefore he saith, Awake thou that sleepest, and arise from the dead, and Christ shall give thee light" (Ephesians 5:14).

Like sleeping Peter, you need to be awakened so that you can have light. Do you remember how, earlier in this book, we looked at the fact that we live in a fallen creation? We crawl to the mirror and gaze at the sight of our puffy eyes, pale face, etc. It's not a pretty sight but one that is most necessary if we want to face people that day. We also need to gaze into the mirror of God's Law. This is most necessary because we have to face Him one day, and if we want to live, we must be morally clean in His sight.

The Moral Law (the Ten Commandments) shows us what we are in truth. Have you ever taken the time to study each of the commandments in the light of its true meaning? Let's do that for a moment. Hold on. A close look in the mirror will not be pleasant, but it is very necessary, so let's do it together.

Answer the following with a tender conscience: Have you ever told a lie? This includes any fibs, white lies, half-truths, or exaggerations you may have told in the past. Remember, time doesn't forgive sin. God sees the sins of your youth as though it were yesterday. If you have told even one lie, then you are a liar. (Be brutally honest with yourself, because God will be honest with you on the Day of Judgment.) Don't pull back from the mirror just because you detect a blemish. Stay close so that you can see yourself clearly.

Have you ever stolen something? The value of the stolen item is totally irrelevant. Let your conscience work for you. Listen to its voice. It was there when you stole. It is a witness to the crime, and its job is to remind you of that fact. (See Romans 2:15.). If you have stolen one thing, then you are a thief.

Have you committed murder, or have you desired to do so by harboring hatred in your heart? If you have hated someone, the Scriptures say that you are a murderer. God sees the thoughts and motives of our hearts.

Jesus said, "Whosoever looketh upon a woman to lust after her hath committed adultery with her already in his heart" (Matthew 5:28). Have you ever done that? Have you had sex outside of marriage, or committed adultery, or desired to? Then you have committed sexual sin and cannot enter Heaven.

Have you kept the Sabbath holy, always honored your parents, and put God first in your affections, loving Him with all your heart, mind, soul, and strength? Have you always loved your neighbor as much as you have loved yourself? Most of us have trouble loving our "loved" ones, let alone loving our neighbors. Have you ever used God's holy name in vain, by either employing it as a filthy curse word, or failing to give it due honor? Have you made a god to suit yourself and therefore been guilty of "idolatry"— making a god in your own image, believing in your version of what you think God is like? Have you ever desired anything that belonged to someone else?

If you have broken even one of these Ten Commandments, then you have sinned against God. On Judgment Day every sin you have ever committed will come out as evidence of your guilt. Every sin you have ever committed is recorded in the corridors of your subconscious mind. You may not be able to instantly recall each of them, but God does. He sees the unclean sexual thoughts. He sees those imaginations you enjoyed, that you thought no one knew about. He has seen the things you have done in darkness, the lies, the things you have stolen, the gossip, and the failure to do what's right. He has watched you as your eyes feasted on that which you knew they shouldn't. Nothing is hidden from His holy and pure eyes. Nothing. Not only has your conscience witnessed your crimes, but God Himself has witnessed them.

If all those thoughts, deeds, and idle words come out as evidence on that Day, you will be damned forever and lose your soul. Without God's mercy, you will go to hell. The thought that that could happen to you horrifies me. Please don't let that happen. Listen to that "impartial judge" in the courtroom of your mind. Don't muffle his voice. What is your conscience saying to you? Is it agreeing with God's Law? Is it doing its God-given duty? I certainly hope so.

Don't add self-righteousness to your sins by saying that you are basically a "good" person. If you refuse to admit that you are guilty, you will never seek God's mercy. Don't think that He will overlook your sins because He is good. As we have seen, His "goodness" will make sure justice is done. He will punish all liars, thieves, adulterers, etc.

Don't be fooled into thinking you can clean up your life. No "good" you do can wash away your sins—only God's mercy can do that. Do you think a judge would dismiss the case of a guilty criminal just because he says that he will clean up his life in the future? Of course he should clean up his life in the future. In the meantime, if he has broken the law, he must be punished.

How do you look in the mirror of God's Law? If you see that you are unclean in the sight of God, then it's time for you to wash. Two thousand years ago, God came to this earth in human form to take the punishment for us. The Bible says, "God commendeth His love toward us, in that, while we were yet sinners, Christ died for us" (Romans 5:8). When Jesus suffered and died on the Cross, He stepped into the courtroom and paid the fine for us. His suffering was necessary to satisfy the Law you and I violated.

Did you see the movie, "The Passion of the Christ"? I did. As I watched the portrayal of all Jesus went through, the palms of my hands began to sweat. I went into hyperventilation during the Crucifixion; it was so brutal. When you see a violent movie, the scene is usually over in a moment, but in "The Passion of the Christ," it went on and on and on. While there was some "artistic license" taken in the movie, the brutality was based on what we are told actually happened to Jesus of Nazareth. It says that He was "marred more than any man." He was "bruised for our iniquities."

Think about what God did for you. He satisfied the Law, and then He cried out, "It is finished!" In other words, the debt had been paid. Then He rose from the dead, defeating death forever. The moment we repent and trust the Savior, God forgives our sins and grants us everlasting life. He justifies us. That means He makes us as though we had never sinned in the first place. He clothes us in the righteousness of His Son.

There are many people who say, "But I confess my sins to God. I tell Him I'm sorry," thinking that this will be enough to grant them entrance into Heaven. If you have those thoughts, think a little more on this. If you find yourself in court with a $50,000 fine, will a judge let you go simply because you say you're sorry and you won't commit the crime again? Of course not. You should be sorry for breaking the law and, of course you shouldn't commit the crime again.

But if someone else pays your $50,000 fine, will you be free from the demands of the law? Of course you will. The judge would say, "This fine has been paid. You're out of here."

God will not forgive you on the basis that you are sorry. Of course we should be sorry for sin—we have a conscience to tell us that adultery, rape, lust, murder, hatred, lying, stealing, etc., are wrong. And of course we shouldn't sin again. However, God will only release us from the demands for eternal justice on the basis that someone else paid our fine. Two thousand years ago, Jesus Christ died on the Cross to pay for the sins of the world.

An Olympic gold-medalist, high-diving champion was once beset with insomnia. As he tossed and turned upon his bed, he began thinking deeply about the success he had attained in his field. He meditated on the gold medals he had won. To his dismay he realized that his success had not achieved what he had hoped. The excitement of winning, the photographers, the medals, and the fame, had given him some sense of pleasure, but the fact of death awaiting him left him with a complete sense of futility.

He rose from the bed and made his way to his diving pool. Because of a full moon, he didn't even bother to turn the lights on. As he climbed the high-diving board, he watched his shadow as it was being cast by the moonlight on the far wall. The routine had become so commonplace to him that he could confidently walk that board in the semi-darkness. At the end of the diving board, he prepared for the dive. He placed his feet together, and then pulled his arms up to a horizontal position. As he did so, his eyes caught a glimpse of his shadow on the far wall. All he could see was a perfect cross. His mind immediately raced back to his

Sunday school days: "God commends his love toward us, in that, while we were yet sinners, Christ died for us." All of a sudden he felt unclean as he considered the commandments he had broken. The sinless Son of God had come to pay the penalty for his sins. He whispered a memory verse he had learned as a child, "For God so loved the world, that He gave His only begotten Son, that whosoever believes on Him should not perish, but have everlasting life." (See John 3:16.)

With tears in his eyes, the great athlete turned around, slowly made his way down to the bottom of the diving board, fell to his knees, and yielded his life to Jesus Christ. He was able to go back to bed and sleep peacefully.

In the morning he arose with a new sense of forgiveness of his sins. He made his way back to the pool, but to his utter astonishment, it was completely empty. The previous evening, the caretaker had emptied it and was just beginning the process of refilling.

Imagine if he had said, "It's true. I am a sinner. I believe that Jesus died for me. Tomorrow I will get right with God ...," and then taken a dive into the empty pool.

A friend of mine named Scotty was once asked by his wife, Carol, to take care of her expensive camera while she went into a store. He sat the bag at his feet, and when she came out of the store some time later, she was horrified to find that he was sound asleep. She picked up the bag and put it behind the seat so that he couldn't see it. Then she woke him up and asked where it was. Scotty was speechless, as well he should have been.

And I'm horrified by the possibility that you could read everything I have just written to you, and not be awakened out of your sleep. I have been trying to stir you with words and if you are not wide awake and alarmed by your terrible plight, it reveals that you don't value your precious life.

If you love your life, then care about your eternal salvation. Don't put it off until tomorrow. That may never come. Today, humbly tell God that you are sorry for your sins, and then show your sincerity by turning from them in repentance. Think of it this way—you are a man who has committed adultery. You have violated the trust of a loving and faithful wife. She is more than willing to forgive you, so how can you reconcile the relationship? You humble yourself, tell her you are truly sorry—then you vow to never (even think of) committing adultery again. You shouldn't need someone to write words of sorrow for you to read to your wife, and you shouldn't have to read a prayer of repentance to God from this book. Just pour your heart out to Him. It's your sincere heart, not the words that really matter.

If you are still not sure what to pray, then make Psalm 51 your prayer. This is King David's apology to God after he sinned against Him by committing adultery with Bathsheba and having her husband murdered:

Have mercy upon me, O God, according to thy lovingkindness: according unto the multitude of thy tender mercies blot out my transgressions. Wash me throughly from mine iniquity, and cleanse me from my sin.

For I acknowledge my transgressions: and my sin is ever before me. Against thee, thee only, have I sinned, and done this evil in thy sight: that thou mightest be justified when thou speakest, and be clear when thou judgest. Behold, I was shapen in iniquity; and in sin did my mother conceive me. Behold, thou desirest truth in the inward parts: and in the hidden part you shall make me to know wisdom. Purge me with hyssop, and I shall be clean: wash me, and I shall be whiter than snow. Make me to hear joy and gladness; that the bones which thou hast broken may rejoice. Hide thy face from my sins, and blot out all mine iniquities. Create in me a clean heart, O God; and renew a right spirit within me. Cast me not away from thy presence; and take not thy holy spirit from me. Restore unto me the joy of thy salvation; and uphold me with thy free spirit. Then will I teach transgressors thy ways; and sinners shall be converted unto thee. Deliver me from bloodguiltiness, O God, thou God of my salvation: and my tongue shall sing aloud of thy righteousness. O Lord, open thou my lips; and my mouth shall shew forth thy praise. For thou desirest not sacrifice; else would I give it: thou delightest not in burnt offering. The sacrifices of God are a broken spirit: a broken and a contrite heart, O God, thou wilt not despise.

After you have confessed your sins to God, put your faith in Jesus as your Lord and Savior. Trust Him in the same way you would trust a pilot with your life when you fly on a plane. The pilot is a fallible man, so how much more should you trust in God? Then read the holy Bible daily, and obey what you read. (See John 14:21.) God will never fail you.

Back to Sleeping Peter

One great sign that you have been truly saved is that you will want to do the will of God. Just after David had cried out to God for mercy, he said, "Then will I teach transgressors thy ways; and sinners shall be converted unto thee" (Psalm 51:13). Seeking to do what God wants will be more important than anything else in your life. Conversion to Christ is to say, "Not my will, but Yours be done."

Remember that as Peter awaited execution, he was bound with chains between two soldiers. More guards stood before the door of the prison. Suddenly an angel of the Lord appeared and stood by him, "and a light shined in the prison." There is a strong inference that the light didn't awaken Peter from his sleep, because the Scriptures then tell us that the angel struck him on the side. As he arose, his chains fell off, he girded himself, tied on his shoes, put on his garment, and followed the angel. After that, the iron gate leading to the city opened of its own accord, and Peter was free.

You were in the prison of your sins. You were taken captive by the devil. You were bound by the chains of sin and were under the sentence of death. You were asleep in your sins. You lived in a dream world. But it wasn't the Gospel light that woke you up. How could the "Good News" alarm you? Rather, the Law struck you. You needed to be struck with the lightning of Mount Sinai and awakened by its terrible thunderings. The Ten Commandments showed you the plight of being on the threshold of death. Then you arose and the Gospel removed the chains of sin and death. It was "the power of God unto salvation" to you. (See Romans 1:16.)

After salvation comes the thanksgiving heart that deeply desires to do the will of Him who saved you from sure death. You will, therefore, gird yourself with truth, tie on your "Gospel shoes," put on your garment of righteousness, follow the Lord, and the iron gate of the Celestial City (Heaven itself) will eventually open of its own accord for you.

Wake-Up Call

God not only wants you to be saved, He wants you to reach out to others with the message of everlasting life. Do you care that all around you are people who, if they die in their sins, will go to hell forever? You should be horrified by this.

Don't be concerned that you aren't "gifted" as a speaker when it comes to reaching this world with the good news of the Gospel. Moses "was learned in all the wisdom of the Egyptians, and was mighty in words and in deeds," yet God didn't use him to deliver Israel until forty years later. It took all that time of tending sheep to produce the necessary meekness of character in him. David writes, "The meek will he guide in judgment: and the meek will he teach his way" (Psalm 25:9).

The "wisdom" that Moses gained in Egypt was not wisdom from above. When he saw injustice, he took the law into his own hands and committed murder. God doesn't need the wisdom of this world. He merely desires a pure, humble, peace-loving, compassionate soul to use as a mouthpiece for the gospel. He wants us to be a lighthouse of His love. The moment we receive the Spirit of Christ, we receive the gift of those virtues. We don't need to tend sheep for forty years when we have the character of the Good Shepherd living through us.

I remember being flown from Los Angeles to the East Coast to do a TV interview when we first came to the U.S. This was a big deal, and I didn't want to blow it. The interviewer began by asking me about my itinerant ministry, so I thought I would establish credibility by letting her know that I was involved in public speaking for a number of years before I began to receive invitations to speak around the country. Unfortunately, instead of saying public speaking, it came out as "public squeaking."

Maybe you don't consider yourself to be very impressive as a spokesperson for God— perhaps you consider yourself to be a "public squeaker." Don't let that stop you. A judge isn't interested in the eloquence of a witness. All he wants is for him or her to speak the truth and to speak it clearly. The Scriptures admonish us to use "great plainness of speech." You want people to be impressed with what you say, not how you say it. I learned this lesson once when I was standing behind my book table when a woman pointed to something on the table and asked, "How much is this?" It was only three dollars, so I simply said, "Three."

She thought I said, "Free," so she picked it up, said, "Thanks," and walked off with it in her hand.

Plane Speaking

Let me share with you how God prepares the hearts of the unsaved. My son-in-law (EZ) and I entered a plane heading for Los Angeles. There was a flight attendant standing at the doorway of the 747, so I showed her my ID. Actually, it's a computer-altered picture in my wallet of my face, but in this photo my forehead is stretched about ten inches higher than it should be. She almost collapsed. She leaned against the wall of the plane, smiled, and said, "Oh, I needed that. I am so tired. Thank you."

I handed her a million-dollar bill gospel tract and said, "Here's a million dollars. You are doing a great job." I had a "What Hollywood Believes"[10] CD in my bag, so I handed it to another flight attendant to give to her. A few minutes later, she plunked herself down in the empty seat beside me and said, "I'm trying to go to Heaven, but I'm afraid I will get off the right path."

I asked her if she thought that she was a good person. Predictably, she did. She was "asleep" as to her terrible plight, so I took her through the Ten Commandments, the Cross, and the necessity of repentance and faith. I also told her that God would give her a new heart with new desires, and that would keep her on the right path. Then I said, "When are you going to surrender, Teresa?" I followed this question with a gentle request, "Let me pray for you."

As we prayed, I thanked God that Teresa had been open to talking about the things of God. I prayed that He would remind her of her past sins, the ones she was ashamed of, and that He would show her how His anger was upon her, that He would reveal the Cross to her and His love for her. Then I also prayed for His blessing of health for her family, and that they, too, would come to know Him.

She looked at me and asked, "Do people become fearful? I'm feeling fear right now." She then said that she had better go and check on the crew.

While she was away, I found a New Testament in my bag and marked the passage in John 3 about how we love the darkness and hate the light. We cringe in fear of the light exposing us. About ten minutes later, back she came once again and sat herself in the seat next to me.

I then explained John 3—that any criminal who sat next to a police officer should feel fear—especially when that officer was exposing her crimes. The light of God's Law is what exposes us. It "smites" us. When that happens, we tend to want to run back to the cover of darkness to hide from the light. Teresa then looked at me and said, "Even though I feel fear, I'm envious of what you've got. Can I really change?"

I leaned across to EZ and told him what she had just said to me. He leaned over towards her and said, "I changed. I was a gang member. I was in the Cripps—a liar and a thief. When I believed in the death and resurrection of the Son of God, I changed. It all went away in an instant—the lying, the theft, and the immorality. I'm now a pastor. Would you sell one of your eyes for a million dollars?"

"No."

"Would you sell both for one hundred million?"

"No."

"Then how much more is your soul worth?"

Teresa looked very sober and said, "That's powerful."

I turned towards her, looked her in the eye, and said, "There's a battle going on for your soul. The devil doesn't want to lose you. When you want to pray, come back and see me."

She stood up and walked down the aisle, obviously under heavy conviction of sin. EZ and I bowed in prayer and asked for God to save her.[11]

Can you see how giving a woman one small gospel tract opened the doors to speak to her about the most important issue of her life—her eternal salvation? Please don't think that you are inadequate to reach out to the lost. Don't worry if you can't answer someone's question. Just say, "I don't know the answer to that, but I will try and find out for you." If you love God and care about this world as it sleeps on the brink of death and hell, then reach out to them today. They may not have tomorrow.

Restless Legs

I trust that you are now right with God and that you want to do His will. Let's go back to the subject of natural sleep for a moment and look at something that can keep us awake.

For years I thought I was the only person on earth who just about went crazy with an excess of energy in my legs when I was trying to get to sleep. It is difficult to explain, but it felt like my legs wanted to do their own thing. They became restless when the rest of my body wanted to rest. It was so strong, I would often have to get out of bed and try and burn off the energy. This was even stronger when I ate or drank anything with sugar in it before I went to bed.

Then I found out that my daughter had similar symptoms. So did my mother and my uncle and aunt. I came to the conclusion that I simply belonged to a strange family! One day in 2005, I saw a TV advertisement for something called "Restless Legs Syndrome" (RLS) and "Periodic Limb Movement Disorder" (PLMD). It was then that I learned that what I had was a common neurological movement disorder that affects as many as twelve million Americans. I further learned:

> "Because the unpleasant feelings occur at rest and are relieved by movement, RLS sufferers have difficulty sleeping. In the NSF 2002 Sleep in America poll, 18% of the female adult population reported RLS symptoms a few nights a week or more. Due to difficulties sleeping, RLS can lead to daytime sleepiness, mood swings, anxiety and depression. One study found that 42% of those with RLS stated that it affected their relationship with their partner. Although we do not know the exact cause of RLS, recent research indicates that iron or folate deficiency may be a risk factor. Treatment may include iron or vitamin supplements, lifestyle changes and medications. About

80% of those with RLS also have PLMD or involuntary leg twitching or jerking movements during sleep that can occur every 20-30 seconds. These symptoms can be bothersome to a bed partner, but are also treatable."

We live in a society in which the word "treatable" means that there is a drug that will help you. It may help you, but more often than not the side effects of modern medicines are worse than the original complaint. So it pays to read the fine print before you put any drug into your body. It amazes me how so many people say that they have no faith in God, but they have so much faith in doctors and the medical profession that they will swallow a drug that could kill them without a second thought. I guess they don't know that "medical mistakes" are the eighth leading cause of death in the United States!

According to a recent report by the Institute of Medicine, medical errors are responsible for at least 44,000 deaths each year in the United States and possibly as many as 98,000 each year. This means that more people die from medical mistakes each year than from breast cancer, highway accidents, or AIDS, the report noted.

The report entitled "To Err is Human" was released by the Institute of Medicine which is part of the National Academy of Sciences, a private organization created by Congress to advise government on scientific matters.

"These stunningly high rates of medical errors resulting in deaths, permanent disability, and unnecessary suffering are simply unacceptable in a medical system that promises to 'do no harm,'" says William Richardson, Chair of the Committee that wrote the report and President and Chief Executive Officer of the W.K. Kellogg Foundation, Battle Creek, Michigan.

According to the report, medical mistakes occur not only in hospitals but in day surgery and outpatient clinics, retail pharmacies, nursing homes, and home care. The report states that medication errors alone contribute to more than 7,000 deaths annually, exceeding those resulting from workplace injuries.[12]

Look at the typical baggage that comes with a popular sleeping pill:[13]

The company that manufactures it warns: All medicines have side effects. Sleep medicines may cause a special type of memory loss or "amnesia." Sleep medicines can cause dependence in some people, especially when these medicines are used regularly for longer than a few weeks or at high doses. All people taking sleep medicines have some risk of becoming dependent on the medicine. Withdrawal symptoms may occur when sleep medicines are stopped suddenly after being used daily for a long time. In more severe cases, abdominal and muscle cramps, vomiting, sweating, shakiness, and, rarely, seizures may occur. Some people using sleep medicines have experienced unusual changes in their thinking and/or behavior. These effects are not common. However, they have included:

- More outgoing or aggressive behavior than normal
- Confusion
- Strange behavior
- Agitation

- Hallucinations
- Worsening of depression
- Suicidal thoughts

Rather than resort to drugs for insomnia or to treat Restless Legs Syndrome, I have found that the best way to treat it is to be mindful of what I eat two hours before I go to bed. I try and stay away from sugars or anything that has the potential to turn into energy. If I do get symptoms, I get up, go downstairs and run on the spot, with very high knee lifts. It looks and feels dumb, but if I leave the light off, no one will see me. I do about 180. At 150 I feel as though I'm about to collapse. The muscles in my legs are screaming for me to stop, but I keep going and do another thirty just to make sure that I exhaust every ounce of energy in my restless legs. It works.

If you are elderly or you are stuck in bed and you get RLS, you will have to throw back the covers, pull up your legs towards your torso, and pretend that you are riding a bike. This feels even dumber than high knee lifts. Make sure you pull your knees up to your chest; otherwise you will strain your stomach muscles. This won't work if you are half-hearted about it. Make sure you do it until you can *hear* the muscles in your legs scream. It's better to get it over with, and be free from feeling as though you are going crazy.

There is one problem, though, with the above exercises. They will get rid of the restless legs, but they may wake you up. Restless legs and insomnia are two more bedfellows. Don't let this bother you. Turn on your non-heat lamp. Pull it over to you. Grab the Book of Psalms, read a few chapters, pick up another book and wait for the wave that prepares the way for sleep.

If you are staying awake because you keep thinking of things that you have to do the next day, keep a pen and paper by your bed, write a quick note to remind you of whatever you have to do, then forget it. Almost every morning I find scads of notes on the floor by my bed. These are things that would have kept me awake, but I moved them from my mind to the paper. Then, when I read the note in the morning, they come back to my mind.

Thinking of something that has to be done the next day is often the mind's attempt to go into first gear as it begins its speedy ride. You can put the brakes on by turning the light on and writing yourself a quick note. The problem with that is that it wakes you up from whatever drowsiness you may have been experiencing. But there is an alternative to note-writing. This will save you from turning the light on and it will save you paper, but it will take an effort. Its advantage is that you will be able to stay in the drowsy state and yet you will have made a mental note that you can pick up in the morning.

It is a word-association memory principle. I learned to do this when I was fourteen years old and I've effectively used it hundreds of times during the night. It is the use of a rhyming list. Here's the list: One, sun. Two, shoe. Three, tree. Four, door. Five, hive, Six, sticks. Seven, heaven. Eight, gate, etc. If I have to remember to pick up a book, buy some ice cream, and change a car tire, I simply say, "One sun"—and think of a situation where I see in my mind the sun burning a book. This must be *seen* in the mind. I have to log in a picture of the sun burning a book. Then

I say "Two, shoe"—and picture an ice cream melting in a shoe. Again, there must be a mental image or this will not work. Then I say, "Three, tree" and imagine car tires hanging from a tree. The silly pictures log into the memory bank better than sane ones. When I want to make a "withdrawal" in the morning, all I have to do is say the rhyme, and the memory is immediately recalled. This also sounds a little strange, but many people use this memory principle because it works. Using it can help you avoid being kept awake by thinking of things you have to do.

Missing Legs Syndrome

Many years ago I asked God to cause things to happen to me that I could use as sermon illustrations. There have been times when I regretted that prayer—from the time I caught on fire while making a cup of tea (I wasn't injured), to where I have hung for a second by my wedding ring from the top rung of a ladder. These weren't too much fun at the time, but they made great and vivid sermon illustrations.

Since praying that prayer, my life has become an interesting adventure. Take, for instance, a recent trip I took to Denver, accompanied by my manager, Mark Spence, and Kirk Cameron's parents. We went there for the national Christian Booksellers Convention.

One of my publishers very kindly decided to design the theme of their booth around one of my new books, *Intelligent Design Versus Evolution*. I decided that I would do my part and take Link—our 6' 6" fake gorilla —to Denver. Link is very realistic-looking, and he has a mechanized head which enhances the realism. I didn't trust the workers who handle the baggage to take good care of him, so I purchased a seat for him on the plane.

As we unloaded Link onto the sidewalk at Los Angeles airport, an LAPD squad car with two smiling officers turned on their vehicle's loud speaker and broadcast, "No gorillas allowed on the plane!" I was acutely aware of that fact, after calling eight airlines and asking if we could take a "relative" onto the plane. This was for our TV program and a video called "The Science of Evolution." When they found that my relative was a "real orangutan," each one of the airlines said that he would have to go into the cargo hold. They intuitively knew that an orangutan on a plane could go ape!

We checked in Link's legs, and then wheeled the rest of him through security. Other than people asking for pictures of us together, and two police officers telling us to stop monkeying around, there were no problems. That is, until I placed him on the seat next to me. He didn't fit. His chest was about 55 inches, and so that put his left arm onto my seat.

A few minutes later I saw a sight I could hardly believe. A monster of a man walked down the aisle and sat next to me. He was huge, so huge that I told him I used to make leather jackets and suede coats to order for people, and then I correctly guessed his chest size. This man had a 60" chest! I had been on around 2,000 flights and had never sat next to anyone this big. With Link on one side and him on the other, I felt like a peanut between two fully grown elephants! When the woman in front put her seat back, I didn't have room to even work on my laptop.

"Derek Bigchest" was an atheist who backslid as I talked about proof for God's existence. It turned out that he was another product of the modern gospel. He had tried Jesus in his teenage years, and the world turned out to be more attractive than the life he was promised. I have always maintained that if you address someone's conscience, you won't find yourself going down side tracks like the monkey trail of evolution. A testimony to the power of biblical evangelism was that despite the overwhelming presence of a huge gorilla beside us, the subject of evolution didn't even come up.

Killed With Kindness
On the way to our hotel in Denver, the taxi stopped at some lights. Suddenly my eyes met those of a homeless and hopeless-looking girl. Her sign and her eyes pleaded for help. I didn't have time to question if she was legitimate. I quickly grabbed five dollars and a tract and asked the driver to wind his window down. She stepped up, he passed her the money, and she said a sincere, "Thank you!"

He said, "Be careful!" Then she turned around and was almost struck by a car that was speeding through the now green light. It must have missed her only by inches!

How I thank God that the car didn't strike her. What a horror it would have been to see her die in such a way. And die she would have in an instant, if she had turned to leave just one-half of a second before she did.

It was a vivid reminder of how transient this life is and how speedily death can take any one of us, if God allows it.

The next day I pushed Link onto the busiest escalator I had ever seen. We had arrived at the convention center at opening time, and there must have been 5,000 people in the lobby, all trying to get up the escalator. At the top, I pushed Link forward, but unfortunately a bump at the top caused him to slump to the left and fall off the wheels on which he was traveling. I didn't panic, but the 5,000 people behind me certainly did. It's amazing how human beings begin to yell as they pile up on one another. I quickly pulled Link up, and lifted the wheels over whatever was catching them. It's also amazing how one small man and a slumped gorilla can cause so much havoc in such a short space of time!

What a huge stumbling block evolution is for humanity! It hinders so many from entering the Kingdom of God, that is, until we learn how to evangelize biblically and speak to the human conscience to clear the way.

We set Link up at the publisher's booth. Then we plugged him in and watched his mechanized head turn. It was worth buying him a seat. His presence added class to an already classy booth.

That night, an alarm went off at the hotel in which we were staying. As Mark Spence and I quickly walked down the stairs, two other patrons were on their way up. Over the sound of the alarm we heard them say, "Go back up. The management told us it's a false alarm." Other evacuees believed them, turned around and without question went back up the stairs. Mark and I kept evacuating. Both of us were reminded of how in 2001, thousands were told to stay in Tower Two of the World Trade Center, because there was no danger.

How quickly this world believes it when they are told (despite the alarm of their conscience) that there is no danger when it comes to sin. God is love and all is well. How true this Scripture is—"There is a way which seemeth right unto a man, but the end thereof are the ways of death" (Proverbs 14:12).

The booksellers' convention was predictably tiring. They always are. Authors sign books, and buyers get free copies. Authors hope that the buyers will then buy. Sometimes they do. But amidst the necessary routine, there are always highlights. One was when Tim Lahaye[14] shook my hand and said, "I've been meaning to write and tell you that I *love The Evidence Bible.*"[15] It was a great encouragement.

On the flight back home, Link's legs were lost on the last leg of the journey. Thanks to the incompetence of the airline workers, we had a "missing Link" (partly). This greatly concerned me because we used him each Saturday to help draw a crowd for our open-air preaching, and their incompetence left him without a leg to stand on. A three-foot gorilla doesn't have the pull of one that normally stands head and shoulders above the crowd. The missing legs confirmed that I had made the right decision not to trust the airline with his torso.

During those two days of travel, Link turned more heads than his own head had turned since his conception. I travel with Kirk Cameron, and we are both continually amazed at the power of his celebrity, but Link easily out-turned Kirk. Hundreds of strangers smiled at me as though they knew me, and they took every tract I offered. I gave out hundreds of "Million-Dollar Bills" with only one refusal, and even he was very polite.

So if you want people to take tracts as if they are going out of fashion, don't wait for a celebrity to call you; simply find your own "missing Link" and wheel him through a busy airport.

It Is High Time to Awake

If you have taken that step and have become a Christian, you will know that it is the most incredible event that will ever take place in your life. You have found peace with your Creator. *You have found everlasting life!* God will never leave you nor forsake you. He has brought you this far and He will complete the wonderful work He has begun in you. God knows your every thought, your every care, and your deepest concerns.

Let's now look at some of those possible concerns. First, and of primary concern—do you have "assurance" of your salvation? The Bible says to "make your calling and election sure" (2 Peter 1:10), so, let's go through a short "checklist" to make sure that you are truly saved:

• Are you aware that God became flesh in the person of Jesus Christ? (See 1 Timothy 3:16.) And that He died for the sins of the world?

• Did you come to the Savior because you had sinned?

• Did you "repent" and put your faith in Jesus?

• Are you convinced that He suffered and died on the cross and that He rose again on the third day?

Now take a look at this interesting experience of a man named LeRoy C. Dugan:

> I shall never forget the impact of this truth on my own father. By the grace of God I was the first member of our family to receive Christ. I was, naturally, so excited about what God had done for me that I wanted everyone to hear about it. At the head of the list was my own father. I testified to him repeatedly about Christ and how important it was to put faith in Him. But my words seemed to have little or no effect.
>
> Finally, during a visit home, the conversation turned once more to Christianity, and my father cried out in

frustration, "Believe. Believe! How do you know when you've 'believed' enough?" I didn't know what more to say. Those dear Christians who had helped me after my conversion always said that the formula to pass out to people was, "Only believe and you will be saved."

So, I concluded, since they knew more than I did, this must be the whole message. Yet it was obvious that it was not enough for my father. He tried hard to "believe" but couldn't seem to do it.

When my brief visit ended and I had gone back to Bible College, I heard one of the instructors make a profoundly simple statement: "If a sinner *will not* repent, he *cannot* believe!" I was thunderstruck!

By experience I knew what it was to repent. But by *training* I had been told, "Only believe!"

When the class ended, I rushed to my writing desk and penned a short letter to my Dad. He received it within two days, read it, and took it to work with him after dinner the same day. He testified afterward that he became so restless at his desk that he went off to a men's lounge at the factory so he could somehow compose himself. When he got there he felt the letter in his pocket, pulled it out and began to read. The first thing his eyes fell upon were the words, "If you cannot believe, it is because there is something of which you are not willing to repent."

Now it was his turn to be thunderstruck. Or should I say, "Spirit struck?"

He saw his problem at once, repented of all of his sins and found it delightfully easy to invite Christ into his life. Assurance came at once! And joy! From that moment to his dying day he was an incurable witness to the reality of salvation.

So the biblical order is "repent and believe." Many preach that all you have to do is believe. This is a tragic error that is not only unbiblical in that it pulls Bible verses out of contact, but it becomes a stumbling block for many, and it has filled the Church with false converts. So make sure that you have truly repented and trusted in the Savior alone.

The moment we do that, God acquits us from the Courtroom of Eternal Justice on the grounds that Jesus Christ paid our fine. We are "justified" (made right with God) by His suffering death. God gives us the righteousness of His Son. The

Resurrection of Jesus Christ was God's seal of approval of the fact that His precious blood was sufficient to pay the fine.

Again, think of it this way: You have violated the law and face a $50,000 fine. You tell the judge that you are truly sorry for your crime, but he answers, "So you should be— you have broken the law! Now, can you pay this fine?" He can only acquit you if the fine is paid. If someone else pays your fine, then he can let you go, but he must have "grounds" on which to release you.

Let's now look at some more important principles that can help you grow and at the same time save you a great deal of pain:

1. Feeding on the Word–DAILY Nutrition

A healthy baby has a healthy appetite. If you have truly been "born" of the Spirit of God, you will have a healthy appetite. The Bible says, "As newborn babes, desire the pure milk of the word, that you may grow thereby" (1 Peter 2:2, NKJV). Feed yourself every day without fail.

Job said, "I have treasured the words of His mouth more than my necessary food" (Job 23:12, NKJV). The more you eat, the quicker you will grow, and the less bruising you will have. Speed up the process and save yourself some pain—vow to read God's Word every day, without fail. Say to yourself, "No Bible, no breakfast. No read, no feed." Be like Job, and put your Bible before your belly. If you do that, God promises that you will be like a fruitful, strong, and healthy tree. (See Psalm 1.) Each day, find somewhere quiet, and thoroughly soak your soul in the Word of God.

There may be times when you read through its pages with great enthusiasm, and there may be other times when it seems dry and even boring. But food profits your body whether you enjoy it or not. As a child, you no doubt ate desserts with great enthusiasm. Perhaps vegetables weren't quite as exciting. If you were a normal child, you probably had to be encouraged to eat them at first. Then, as you matured in life, you were taught to discipline yourself to eat vegetables. This is because you knew they would physically benefit you, even though they may not have brought pleasure to your taste buds.

2. Faith–Elevators Can Let You Down

When a young man once looked at me and said, "I find it hard to believe some of the things in the Bible," I smiled and asked, "What's your name?"

When he said, "Paul," I casually answered, "I don't believe you." He looked at me questioningly and I repeated, "What's your name?"

Again, he said, "Paul," and again I answered, "I don't believe you." Then I asked, "Where do you live?" When he told me where he lived, I said, "I don't believe that either."

You should have seen his reaction. He was angry. I said, "You look a little upset. Do you know why? You're upset because I didn't believe what you told me. If you tell me that your name is Paul, and I say, 'I don't believe you,' it means that I think you are a liar. You are trying to deceive me by telling me your name is Paul, when it's not." Then I told him that if he, a mere man, felt insulted by my lack of faith in his word, how much more does he insult Almighty God by refusing to believe His Word. In doing so, he was saying that God isn't worth trusting—that He is a liar and a deceiver. The Bible says, "He who does not believe God has made Him a liar" (1 John 5:10, NKJV). It also says, "Beware, brethren, lest there be in any of you an evil heart of unbelief ... (Hebrews 3:12, NKJV). Martin Luther said, "What greater insult ... can there be to God, than not to believe His promises."

I have heard people say, "But I just find it hard to have faith in God," not realizing the implications of their words. These are the same people who often believe the weather forecast, believe the newspapers, and trust their lives to a pilot they have never seen whenever they fly in a plane. We exercise faith every day. We trust our car's brakes. We trust our history books, our medical books, and we trust elevators. Yet elevators can let us down. History books can be wrong. Planes can crash. How much more then should we trust the sure and true promises of Almighty God? He will never let us down—if we trust Him.

I have often heard cynics say, "The Bible is full of mistakes." It is. The first mistake was when man rejected God, and the Scriptures show men and women making the same tragic mistake again and again. It's also full of what seem to be contradictions. For example, the Scriptures tell us "With God, nothing shall be impossible" (Luke 1:37). We are told that there is nothing Almighty God can't do. Yet we are also told that it is "impossible for God to lie" (Hebrews 6:18). So there is something God cannot do! There's an obvious "mistake" in the Bible. The answer to this dilemma is to be found in the lowly worm.

Do you know that it would be impossible for me to eat worms, although I have seen people eat them. On TV I once saw a man butter his toast, then pour on a can of live, fat, wriggling, blood-filled worms. He carefully took a knife and fork, cut into his moving meal, and ate it. It made me feel sick. It was disgusting. The thought of chewing cold, live worms is so repulsive, so distasteful,

I can candidly say it would be impossible for me to eat them, even though I have seen it done. It is so abhorrent to me that I draw on the strength of the word "impossible" to substantiate my claim.

Lying, deception, bearing false witness, etc., are so repulsive to God, so disgusting to Him, so against His holy character, that the Scriptures draw on the strength of the word "impossible" to substantiate the claim. He cannot, could not, and would not lie.

That means that in a world where we are continually let down, we can totally rely on, trust in, and count on His promises. They are sure, certain, indisputable, true, trustworthy, reliable, faithful, unfailing, dependable, steadfast, and an anchor for the soul. In other words, you can truly believe them, and because of that, you can throw yourself blindfolded and without reserve into His mighty hands. He will never, ever, let you down. Do you believe that?

3. Evangelism–Our Most Sobering Task

It was late in December, 1996. A large family gathered in Los Angeles for the joyous occasion of wrapping Christmas presents. It was a big family because it was the product of two marriages. There were so many gathered that night that five of the children had to sleep in the garage—a converted structure that was kept warm during the cold night by an electric heater which sat by the door.

During the early hours of the morning, the heater suddenly burst into flames, which blocked the doorway. In seconds the room became a blazing inferno. The frantic 911 call revealed the unspeakable terror of the moment. One of the children could be heard screaming, "I'm on fire!" The distraught father vainly rushed into the flames to try and save his beloved children. He received burns on 50 percent of his body. Tragically, all five of the children burned to death! They died because steel bars on the windows of the garage thwarted their escape. There was only one door, and that was stopped by the flames.

Let's go back in time. It's minutes before the heater bursts into flames. You peer through the darkness at the peaceful sight of five sleeping youngsters. You know that at any moment the room is going to erupt into an inferno and burn the flesh of horrified children. Can you in good conscience walk away? No! You must awaken them and warn them to run from that death trap!

The world sleeps peacefully in the darkness of ignorance. There is only one Door by which they may escape death. The steel bars of sin prevent their salvation, and at the same time call for the flames of eternal justice. What a fearful thing Judgment Day will be! The fires of the wrath of Almighty God will burn for eternity. The Church has been entrusted with the task of awakening people before it's too late. We cannot turn our backs and walk away in complacency. Think of how the father ran into the flames. His love knew no bounds, and our devotion to the sober task that God has given us will be in direct proportion to our love for the lost. There are only a few who run headlong into the flames to warn them to flee. (See Luke 10:2.) Please be one of them. We really have no choice. The Apostle Paul said, "Woe is me if I do not preach the gospel!" (1 Corinthians 9:16, NKJV).

When speaking of love, the Scriptures say, "And that, knowing the time, that now it is high time to awake out of sleep: for now is our salvation nearer than when we believed" (Romans 13:11). We have a job to do and we must have a sense of urgency about it.

It was the "Prince of Preachers," Charles Spurgeon, who said, "Have you no wish for others to be saved? Then you are not saved yourself. Be sure of that." A Christian cannot be apathetic about the salvation of the world. The love of God in him will motivate him to seek and save that which is lost.

You probably have a limited amount of time after your conversion to impact your unsaved friends and family with the Gospel. After the initial shock of your conversion, they will put you in a neat little ribbon-tied box, and keep you at arm's length. So it's important that you take advantage of the short time you have while you still have their ears.

Here's some advice that will save you a great deal of grief. As a new Christian, a friend of mine did almost irreparable damage by acting like a wild bull in a crystal showroom. He bullied his mom, his dad, and many of his friends into making a "decision for Christ." He was sincere, zealous, loving, kind, and stupid! He didn't understand that salvation doesn't come through making a "decision," but through repentance, and repentance is God-given. (See 2 Timothy 2:25.)

The Bible teaches that no one can come to the Son unless God "draws" him or her. If you are able to get a decision from someone but that person has no conviction of sin, you will almost certainly end up with a stillborn on your hands.

In his "zeal without knowledge," my friend actually inoculated the very ones he was so desperately trying to reach. There is nothing more important to you than the salvation of your loved ones, and you don't want to blow it. If you do, you may find that you don't have a second chance. Fervently pray for them, thanking God for their salvation. Let them see your faith. Let them feel your kindness, your genuine love, and your gentleness. Buy gifts for no reason. Do chores when you are not asked to. Go the extra mile. Put yourself in their position. You know that you have found everlasting life. Death has lost its sting! Your joy is unspeakable—but as far as they are concerned, you have been brainwashed. You have become part of a weird sect. So your loving actions will speak more loudly than 10,000 eloquent sermons ever could.

It is because of these thoughts that you should hold back from verbal confrontation until you have knowledge that will guide your zeal. Pray for wisdom and for sensitivity to God's timing. You may have only one shot, so make it count. Keep your cool. If you don't, you may end up with a lifetime of regret. Believe me, it is better to hear a loved one or a close friend say, "Tell me about your faith in Jesus Christ," rather than you saying, "Sit down. I want to talk to you."

It is important to realize that we should share our faith with others whenever we can. The Bible says that there are only two times when we should do this—"... in season and out of season" (2 Timothy 4:2). The Apostle Paul pleaded for prayer for his own personal witness. He said, "... that utterance may be given unto me, that I may open my mouth boldly, to make known the mystery of the gospel, for which I am an ambassador in bonds: that therein I may speak boldly, as I ought to speak" (Ephesians 6:19-20).

Remember that you have the sobering responsibility of speaking to other people's loved ones. Many times when you open your mouth to speak the Gospel, you may be the answer to the earnest prayer of another Christian. Perhaps the other person has cried out to God that He would use a faithful witness to speak to his or her beloved mom or dad, and you are the answer to that prayer. You are that "true and faithful witness" that God wants to use.

Never lose sight of the world and all its pains. Keep the fate of the ungodly before your eyes. Too many of us settle down on a padded pew and become introverted. Our world becomes a monastery without walls. Our friends are confined solely to those within the Church, when Jesus was the "friend of sinners." So take the time to deliberately befriend unbelievers for the sake of their salvation. Remember that each and every person who dies in their sins has an appointment with the Judge of the universe. Hell opens wide its terrible jaws. There is no more sobering task than to be entrusted with the Gospel of Salvation—working with God for the eternal well-being of dying humanity.

4. Prayer—"Wait For a Minute."

It has been well said that God always answers prayer. Sometimes He says, "Yes." Sometimes He says, "No." Sometimes He says, "Wait for a minute." Remember that a day to the Lord is as a thousand years to us. (See 2 Peter 3:8.) That means that a ten-year wait for us, is 14 minutes and 24 seconds to God, so ask in faith, but rest in peace-filled patience.

Surveys show that more than 90 percent of Americans pray daily. No doubt they pray for health, wealth, happiness, etc. They also pray when grandma gets sick, and when grandma doesn't get better (or dies), many end up feeling disillusioned, and some end up bitter. This is because they don't understand what the Bible says about prayer. It teaches that sin will stop God from even hearing your prayer. (See Psalm 66:18.) It teaches, among other things, that if we pray with doubt, we will not get an answer. (See James 1:6-7.)

Here's how to be heard ...

1.) Pray with faith. (See Hebrews 11:6.)

2.) Pray with clean hands and a pure heart. (See Psalm 24:3-4.)

3.) Pray genuine, heart-felt prayers, rather than vain repetitions. (See Matthew 6:7.)

4.) Make sure that you are praying to the God who is revealed in the Holy Scriptures. (See Exodus 20:3-6.)

How do you "pray with faith?" If someone says to you, "You're a man of great faith in God," they may think that they are paying you a compliment. But they aren't—the compliment is actually addressed to God. For example, if I said to you, "I'm a man of great faith in my doctor," it's actually the doctor I'm complimenting. If I have great faith in him, it means that I see him as a man of integrity, a man of great ability—that he is trustworthy. I give "glory" to the man through my faith in him.

The Bible says that Abraham "... did not waver at the promise of God through unbelief, but was strengthened in faith, giving glory to God, and being fully convinced that what He had promised He was also able to perform" (Romans 4:20-21, NKJV). Abraham was a man of great faith in God. Remember, that is not a compliment to Abraham. He merely caught a glimpse of God's incredible ability, His impeccable integrity, and His wonderful faithfulness to keep every promise He makes. His faith gave "glory" to a faithful God.

As far as God is concerned, if you belong to Jesus, you are a VIP. You can boldly come before the throne of Grace. (See Hebrews 4:16.) You have access to the King, because you are the son or daughter of the King. When you were a child, did you have to grovel to get your needs met by your mom or dad? I hope not.

So, when you pray, don't say, "Oh, God, I hope you will supply my needs." Instead, say something like, "Father, thank you that you keep every promise You make. Your Word says that you will supply all my needs according to Your riches in glory, by Christ Jesus. (See Philippians 4:19.) Therefore, I thank you that you will do this thing for my family. I ask this in the wonderful name of Jesus. Amen"

It was the great missionary, Hudson Taylor, who said, "The prayer power has never been tried to its full capacity. If we want to see Divine power wrought in the place of weakness, failure, and disappointment, let us answer God's standing challenge, 'Call unto me, and I will answer you, and show thee great and mighty things of which you know not of.'" (Jeremiah 33:3)

How do you get "clean hands and a pure heart"? Simply by confessing your sins to God through Jesus Christ. His blood cleanses us from all sin. (See 1 John 1:7-9.) When you confess your sins to God through Jesus, God will not only forgive your every sin, He promises to forget those sins as well. (See Hebrew 8:12.) He will even justify you on the grounds of the sacrifice that was made by the Savior. That means He will count it as though you have never sinned in the first place. He will make you pure in His sight— sinless. He will even "purge" your conscience, so that you will no longer have that sense of guilt that you sinned in the first place. That's what I mean "to be justified by faith." That's why you need to soak yourself in the holy Scriptures—to read the letters to the churches and see the wonderful things God has done for us through the Cross of Calvary. If you don't bother to read the will, you won't have any idea of what has been left to you.

How do you pray "genuine heart-felt prayers"? Simply by keeping yourself in the love of God. If the love of God is in you, you will never pray hypocritical or selfish prayers. In fact, you won't have to pray selfish prayers, if you have a heart of love. When your prayer-life is pleasing to God, the Bible says that He will reward you openly. (See Matthew 6:6.)

How do you know that you are praying to "the God revealed in holy Scripture"? Study the Word. Don't accept the image of God that is portrayed by the world, even though it appeals to the natural mind. A loving, kind, fatherly figure, with no sense of justice or truth appeals to guilty sinners. Look to the thundering's and lightning's of Mount Sinai. Gaze at Jesus on the Cross of

Calvary–hanging there in unspeakable agony because of the justice of a holy God. Such thoughts tend to banish idolatry.

5. Warfare–Praise the Lord and Pass the Ammunition

When you became a Christian, you stepped right into the heat of an age-old battle. You have a three-fold enemy—the world, the flesh, and the devil. Before you became a Christian, you floated downstream with the other dead fish. But now, God has put His life within you, and you will find yourself swimming against a three-fold current. Let's look at these three resistant enemies.

First, the world. When the Bible speaks of the "world" in this context, it is referring to the sinful, rebellious world system. This is the world that loves the darkness and hates the light. (See John 3:20.) It is governed by the "god of this world." (See 2 Corinthians 4:4.) The "god of this world" is also known as the "prince of the power of the air" (Ephesians 2:2).

The Bible says the Christian has escaped the corruption that is in the world through lust. "Lust" is unlawful desire, and is the life blood of the world—whether it be in the form of lust for sexual sin, for power, for money, or for material things. Lust is a monster that will never be gratified, so don't even attempt to feed it. It will grow bigger and bigger if you do, until it weighs heavy upon your back, and ultimately it will be the death of you! (See James 1:15.)

In and of themselves there is nothing wrong with sex, power, money, or material things, but when these become predominant in God's sight, the Bible calls them "inordinate affections." (See Colossians 3:5.) We are told, "Do not love the world or the things in the world. If anyone loves the world, the love of the Father is not in him" (1 John 2:15, NKJV).

"Whoever therefore wants to be a friend of the world makes himself an enemy of God" (James 4:4, NKJV).

The second enemy is the devil. As we have seen, he is known as the "god of this world." He was your spiritual father before you joined the family of God. (See John 8:44 and

Ephesians 2:2.) Jesus called the devil a thief, who came to kill, steal, and destroy. (See John 10:10.)

The way to overcome him and his demons is to make sure you are outfitted with the spiritual armor of God that is outlined and listed in Ephesians 6:10-20. Become intimately familiar with it. Sleep in it. Never take it off. Bind the two-edged sword to your hand so that you never lose its grip. This brings us to the third enemy.

The third enemy is what the Bible calls the "flesh." This is your sinful nature and the battlefield of your mind.

If you have a mind to, you will be attracted to the world and all its sin. The mind is the data-processing control panel for the eyes and the ears. It is the center of your appetites. All sin begins in the "heart." (See Proverbs 4:23 and Matthew 15:19.) We think before we sin. This actually happens because we don't think before we sin. The Bible warns that lust brings forth sin, and sin when it's conceived, brings forth death. Every day of our lives, we have a choice to sin or not to sin—that is the question. The answer to the question of sin is the fear of God. If you don't fear God, you will sin to your sinful heart's delight.

Did you know that God sometimes kills people? He killed a man because he didn't like what he did sexually. (See Genesis 38:10.) He killed a husband and wife because they told just one lie. (See Acts 5:1-11.) Knowledge of God's goodness—His righteous judgments against evil—should put the fear of God in us and help us not to indulge in sin.

If we know that the eye of the Lord is in every place beholding the evil and the good, and that He will bring every work to judgment, we will live accordingly. Such weighty thoughts are valuable, for "by the fear of the LORD one departs from evil" (Proverbs 16:6, NKJV).

Jesus said, "And I say to you, My friends, do not be afraid of those who kill the body, and after that have no more that they can do. But I will show you whom you should fear: Fear Him who, after He has killed, has power to cast into hell; yes, I say to you, fear Him!" (Luke 12:4-5).

6. *Fellowship–Flutter by Butterfly*

Pray about where you should fellowship with other believers. Make sure the place you are going to call your church home calls sin what it is—sin. Do they believe the promises of God? Are they loving? Does the pastor treat his wife with respect? Is he a man of the Word? Does he have a humble heart and a gentle spirit? Listen closely to his teaching. It should glorify God, magnify Jesus, and edify the believer. One evidence that you have been truly saved is that you will have a love for other Christians. (See 1 John 3:14.) You will want to fellowship with them.

The old saying that "birds of a feather flock together" is true of Christians. You gather together for the breaking of bread (communion), for teaching from the Word, and for fellowship. You share the same inspirations, illuminations, inclinations, temptations, aspirations, motivations, and perspirations—you are working together for the same thing, for the furtherance of the Kingdom of God on earth. This is why you attend church—not because you have to, but because you want to.

Don't become a "spiritual butterfly." Send your roots down. If you are moving from church to church, how will your pastor know what type of food you are digesting? The Bible says that your shepherd will have to give an account to Him that has entrusted you to him (See Hebrews 13:17.), so make yourself known to your pastor. Pray for him regularly. Pray also for his wife, his family, and the elders. Being a pastor is no easy task.

Most people don't realize how many hours it takes to gather a fresh sermon each week. They don't appreciate the time spent in prayer and the study of the Word. If the pastor makes the same joke twice, or shares something he has shared before, remember, he's human. So give him a great deal of grace and double honor. Never murmur about him. If you don't like something he has said, pray about it, then leave the issue with God. If that doesn't satisfy you, leave the church, rather than divide it through murmuring and complaining.

A woman once spread some hot gossip about a local pastor. What he had supposedly done became common knowledge around town. Then she found that what she had heard wasn't true. She gallantly went to the pastor and asked for his forgiveness. The pastor forgave her, but then told her to take a pillow full of tiny feathers to a corner of the town, and in high winds, shake the feathers out. Then he told her to try and pick up every feather. He explained that the damage had already been done. She had destroyed his good reputation and trying to repair the damage was like trying to pick up feathers in high winds.

The Bible says that there is life and death in the power of the tongue. We can kill or make something alive with our words. The Scriptures also reveal that God hates those who cause division among the brethren. (See Proverbs 6:19.) Pray with the Psalmist, "Set a guard, O Lord, over my mouth; keep watch over the door of my lips" (Psalm 141:3, NKJV).

Remember the old saying, "He that gossips to you, will gossip about you."

7. *Thanksgiving–Do the Right Thing*

For the Christian, every day should be Thanksgiving Day. We should even be thankful in the midst of problems. The Apostle Paul said, "I am exceedingly joyful in all our tribulation" (2 Corinthians 7:4, NKJV). He knew that God was working all things together for his good, even though he was going through trials. (See Romans 8:28.)

Problems will come your way. God will see to it personally that you grow as a Christian. He will allow the storms, so that you will send your roots deep into the soil of His Word. We pray more in the midst of problems, and it's been well said that you will see more from your knees, than you will on your tiptoes.

A man once watched a butterfly struggling to get out of its cocoon. In an effort to help it, he took a razor blade, and carefully slit the edge of the cocoon. The butterfly escaped from its problem—and immediately died!

It is God's way to have the butterfly struggle. It is the struggle that causes its tiny heart to beat fast, and send the life's blood into its wings.

Trials have their purpose. They make us struggle—they bring us to our knees. They are the cocoon in which we often find ourselves. It is there that the life's blood of faith in God helps us spread our wings.

Faith and thanksgiving are close friends. If you have faith in God, you will be thankful because you know His loving hand is upon you, even though you are in a lion's den. That will give you a deep sense of joy, and joy is the barometer of the depth of faith you have in God.

Let me give you an example. Imagine if I said I would give you one million dollars if you sent me an e-mail. Of course, you don't believe that I would do that. But imagine if you did. Imagine if you had knowledge of more than 1,000 people who had sent me an e-mail, and every one received their million dollars—no strings attached. Let's go a bit further: You had actually called me, and I had assured you personally that I would keep my word. If you believed me, wouldn't you have joy? If you didn't believe me—no joy. The amount of joy you have would be a barometer as to how much you believed my promise.

We have so much to be thankful for. God has given us "exceeding great and precious promises" that are "more to be desired than gold." Do yourself a big favor— believe those promises, thank God continually for them, and "let your joy be full."

An old farmer once had an ungodly relative visit him. After the farmer had bowed his head and thanked God for the food they were about to eat, the relative rudely said, "What did you do that for? There's no God. We live in an age of enlightenment."

The old farmer smiled and said, "There is one on the farm who doesn't thank God before he eats."

The relative sat up and said, "Who is this enlightened one?"

The farmer quietly replied, "My pig."

8. *Water Baptism–Sprinkle or Immerse?*

The Bible says, "Repent, and be baptized, every one of you in the name of Jesus Christ for the remission of sins …" (Acts 2:38). There is, therefore, no question as to whether or not you should be baptized. The questions are how, when, and by whom?

It would also seem clear from Scripture that those who were baptized were fully immersed in water. Here's one reason why: "And John also was baptizing in Aenon near to Salim, because there was much water there …" (John 3:23).

If John was merely sprinkling believers, he would have only needed a cup full of water.

The Philippian jailer and his family were baptized at midnight, as soon as they believed. So what are you waiting for?

Who should baptize you? It is clear from Scripture that other believers have the privilege to do so, but check with your pastor, for he may want the honor himself.

9. Giving, the Last Frontier

It was once said that the wallet is the "last frontier." It is the final area to be conquered—the last thing that comes to God in surrender. Jesus spoke much about money. He said that we cannot serve both God and mammon. (See Matthew 6:24.) The word "mammon" was the common Aramaic word for riches, which is akin to a Hebrew word signifying "that which is to be trusted." In other words, we cannot trust both God and money. Either money is our source of life, our great love, our joy, our sense of security, the supplier of our needs—or God is.

When you open your purse or wallet, give generously and regularly to your local church. Give because you want to, not because you have to. God loves a cheerful giver (see 2 Corinthians 9:7), so learn to hold your money with a loose hand.

10. Troubleshooting Cults, Atheists, and Skeptics

If you know the Lord, nothing will shake your faith. It is true that the man with an experience is not at the mercy of a man with an argument. Take, for example, a little boy who is looking at a heater. His father warns him that it's hot. The child says, "O.K. I believe it's hot." At that point, he has an intellectual belief that the heater is hot. When his dad leaves the room, he says, "I wonder if it really is hot?" He then reaches out his little hand and grabs the heater bar with his fingers. The second his flesh burns, he stops believing the heater is hot. He now knows it's hot! He has moved out of the realm of "faith" into the realm of "experience."

In comes a heater expert and says, "Son, I have a B.A. in the study of heat. The heater is definitely not hot. I can prove it to you."

In such a case the child would probably say, "Mr. Expert, I don't care how many B.A.'s you have. I know that heater is hot— I touched it! I'm not in the realm of belief, I'm in the realm of experience. Goodbye."

If you have touched the heater bar of God's love and forgiveness, if the Holy Spirit has "born witness" that you are a child of God (See Romans 8:16.), if you have received the Gospel with "power, the Holy Ghost and much assurance" (See 1 Thessalonians 1:5.), and if you are converted, you will never be shaken by a skeptic.

When cults tell you that you must acknowledge God's name to be saved, that you must worship on a certain day, or that you must be baptized by an elder of their church, don't panic. Merely go back to "the Instruction Manual." The Bible has all the answers, and searching them out will make you grow. If you feel intimidated by atheists—if you think they are "intellectuals"—read my book *God Doesn't Believe in Atheists*. It will reveal to you that they are not so intimidating after all. It will also show you how to prove God's existence and also prove that the "atheist" doesn't exist.

Finally, the way to prevent sporting injury and pain is to keep yourself fit. Exercise. The Apostle Paul kept spiritually fit through exercise. He said, "Herein do I exercise myself, to have always a conscience void of offence toward God, and toward men" (Acts 24:16). You must do the same. Listen to the voice of your conscience. It's your friend, not your enemy.

Remember these words of Solomon: "Fear God, and keep his commandments: for this is the whole duty of man. For God shall bring every work into judgment, with every secret thing, whether it be good or whether it be evil" (Ecclesiastes 12:13-14). Keep the Day of Judgment before your eyes. On that day, you will be glad that you cultivated a tender conscience. I hope these principles have been helpful and that they will some day save you some pain.

In Conclusion

Oh, how I hope you are right with God. If you are, you have no reason to lay awake at night. You don't need to be anxious even if you know that you will die tomorrow. You may not know what the next day holds, but you know the One who holds the next day in His mighty hands. He is the Lover of your soul, and not one hair on your head will perish, because of that great love. Take the time to read Romans 8, and personalize it to yourself.

If you do have restless nights, don't take any notice of alarmists who say you will go insane if you don't get a good night's sleep. Don't forget about that man who went for twelve days without a wink, and he kept his sanity. Napoleon, Michelangelo, Florence

Nightingale, Margaret Thatcher, Martha Stewart, and the entire research team of Thomas Edison got by on four hours of sleep a night (also remember that Edison thought that sleep was a complete waste of time). Edgar Allan Poe didn't think that sleep was a waste of time. He hated it. He said of sleep, "Those little slices of death, how I loathe them." Leonardo Da Vinci is said to have slept for fifteen minutes every four hours.

The University of Texas Southwestern Medical Center at Dallas notes in its

Health Watch: "As long as people got more than four hours of sleep a night, they didn't have an increased risk of dying. Oddly enough, people who slept more than eight hours a night had a slightly higher risk for death than those who got only seven hours of sleep a night. There was also an increased risk associated with using sleeping pills."

The McKinley Health Center, in an article titled, "On Insomnia and Other Related Sleep Problems," added, "Requirements for sleep vary widely. Most adults need the traditional seven or eight hours of sleep a night, but some adults are 'short sleepers' and function well on only three or four hours. Many people overestimate the amount of sleep they need and underestimate the amount they actually get during a restless night. Generally there is no need for concern, even if an unbroken night's sleep is rare. However if loss of sleep impairs a person's ability to function well during the day, it might indicate a problem."

So, according to these experts, if you can't sleep, it won't kill you. However, worry will. Therefore, make sure that you love and trust God with all of your heart. Don't worry about a thing. Give it all to God in prayer. Here's a summary of points that may be helpful:

• Try to go to sleep at the same time each night and get up at the same time each morning. Do not take afternoon naps. Sometimes the temptation to do so can be overwhelming. Get up and do something active, and the temptation will more than likely leave.

• Experts say to avoid caffeine, nicotine, and alcohol late in the day or at night. I would suggest that you avoid the poisons of nicotine and alcohol *all the time* (duh!).

• Get regular exercise. Exercise during the day—make sure you exercise at least five to six hours before bedtime.

• Make sure you eat dinner at least two to three hours before bedtime.

• Keep your bedroom dark, quiet, and cool. If light is a problem, try a sleeping mask. If noise is a problem, try earplugs, a fan, or a "white noise" machine to cover up the sounds.

• Follow a routine to help relax and wind down before sleep, such as reading a book, listening to music, or taking a bath.

• If you lay awake worrying about things, write what you have to do the next day on a note.

• Stay away from sugar before you go to bed.

• Read your Bible each day, and whenever you can, spend your waking hours reaching out to the lost.

Thanks for taking the time to read this book. I hope that what I have said has been helpful. Now, if it's the right time to do so, go and get some sleep.

something we will look at in a later chapter.

Footnotes

[1] See, *The Evidence Bible* (Bridge Logos publishers).

[2] Unless it's "Restless Legs Syndrome," something we will look at in a later chapter.

[3] See *The Evidence Bible* (Bridge Logos Publishers).

[4] www.biblegateway.com/

[5] See 2 Timothy 3:16

[6] http://en.wikipedia.org/wiki John_A.T._Robinson

[7] John 8:44, Ephesians 5:6, Colossians 3:6, 1 John 3:10

[8] Matthew 7:21-24

[9] See John 3:3

[10] These products are available though
<u>www.livingwaters.com</u> or by calling 1(800)
437-1893

[11] Don't miss *Thanks a Million!* by Ray
Comfort and Kirk Cameron. This book is
packed with real life witnessing situations.

[12] http://www.freecasereview.com/
InjuryLawArticles/medicalerrors.htm

[13] http://www.lunesta.com/lunestaOverview/
lunestaPPI.html

[14] Co-author of the *Left Behind* books which
has sold more than 50,000,000 copies.

[15] This is available through
<u>www.livingwaters.com</u>

"The Way of the Master"
Evidence Bible

Prove God's existence. Answer 100 common objections to Christianity. Show the Bible's supernatural origin. This unique study Bible includes wisdom from the foremost Christian leaders of yesterday and today such as Charles Spurgeon, D.L. Moody, John Wesley, Charles Finney, George Whitefield, Billy Graham, Dr. Bill Bright, John MacArthur, and R.C. Sproul.

Complete Bible available in
- Hardback
- Leather-bound (black or burgundy)
- Paperback

New Testament, Proverbs & Pslams available in
- Paperback
- Black leather-bound pocket editon

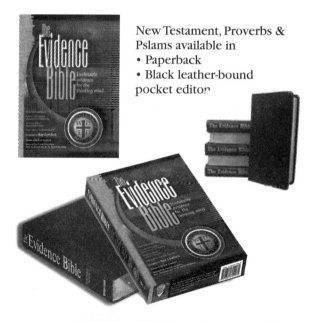

More **Bridge-Logos** Titles
from Ray Comfort

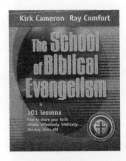

The School of Biblical Evangelism

In this comprehensive study course, you will learn how to share our faith simply, effectively, and biblically … the way Jesus did. Discover the God-given evangelistic tools that will enable you to confidently talk about the Savior.

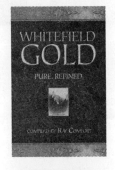

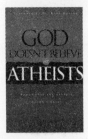

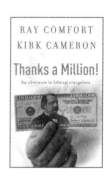

AVAILABLE AT FINE CHRISTIAN BOOKSTORES

OTHER BOOKS BY RAY COMFORT

DON T MISS

Springboards for Budding Preachers
(comes with fsix DVDs)

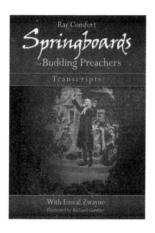

Twenty-eight live, open-air, Gospel messages
by Ray Comfort

For more than two and a half years, Ray Comfort and Emeal Zwayne (General Manager of The Way of the Master and Living Waters Publications) preached the Gospel in the open air to the crowds waiting daily outside the courtroom in Bellflower, California. During that time, an estimated 30,000 people heard the Gospel.

On September 30, 2005, a Los Angeles County judge issued a court order forbidding public speaking, affecting not only this court but the grounds of more than forty courtrooms in L.A. County, despite the fact that it is public soil. Fortunately, our sound man, Stuart Scott, recorded the last twenty-eight days of the preaching. These messages are packed with illustrations and springboards for open-air preachers, so you can learn how to speak boldly while we still have the opportunity to do so.

For More Information about Ray Comfort

visit www.livingwaters.com
call 1(800) 437-1893
or write to:
Living Waters Publications
P.O. Box 1172
Bellflower, CA 90706, USA